Sunset

ideas for great
BATHROOMS

By the Editors of
Sunset Books

Sunset Books ■ Menlo Park, California

Sunset Books

vice president, general manager:
Richard A. Smeby

vice president, editorial director:
Bob Doyle

Lory Day

art director:
Vasken Guiragossian

Staff for this book:

developmental editor:
Linda J. Selden

book editor:
Scott Atkinson

copy editor:
Marcia Williamson

design:
Barbara Vick

illustrations:
Mark Pechenik

principal photographer:
Philip Harvey

photo director:
JoAnn Masaoka Van Atta

production coordinator:
Patricia S. Williams

1 0   9

*ISBN 0-376-01319-2
Library of Congress Catalog Card Number: 98-86385
Printed in the United States.*

For additional copies of Ideas for Great Bathrooms or any other Sunset book, call 1-800-526-5111, or visit our website at: www.sunsetbooks.com

Cover: An arched opening frames a bath area dressed with warm pine woodwork, cool marble, and rough-textured yellow plaster on walls and ceiling. Interior designer: Osburn Design of San Francisco. Architect: David Williams. Cover design by Vasken Guiragossian. Photography by Philip Harvey. Photo direction by JoAnn Masaoka Van Atta.

Wade right in...

The bathroom, once ignored or maligned, is becoming a haven of both comfort and style. Plot the bath of your dreams with this newly revised Sunset title as your guide. You'll find the latest in both gleaming fixtures and efficient designs. From a cozy armchair, you can examine scores of striking bath installations in full color. Or see what's available in European cabinets, whirlpool tubs, ultra-low-flush toilets, and low-voltage downlights. If you're ready to dig in, you'll also find a solid introduction to bathroom planning.

Many professionals and homeowners provided information and encouragement or allowed us to take a look at their new installations. We'd especially like to thank The Plumbery and The Bath and Beyond of San Francisco. Our thanks also go to Chugrad McAndrews, who spent many hours ably assisting with location photography.

Design credits for specific photos are listed on pages 110–111.

contents

Make a
big splash

THE WORD is out: people today want bathrooms to be bold, beautiful, and—especially—comfortable.

It wasn't always that way. The first wooden bathtubs, scenes of the painfully elaborate Saturday-night scrubs immortalized by Western movies, appeared in the mid-1800s. Soon these leaky vessels were replaced by cast-iron tubs—essentially horse troughs with legs. The bathroom as we know it came indoors only in the 1920s, and with no great fanfare. Health and privacy concerns, not aesthetics, prompted the move.

A new but mandatory 5- by 7-foot space—a "terra incognita"—now appeared on architects' and tract-builders' plans.

Today, whether due to the development of two-earner families, to greater stress in the outside world, or simply to the whims of the "me" generation, homeowners are asking their architects and designers to give new thought to the use of this space. The bathroom is no longer an out-of-sight, out-of-mind proposition; it's a rewarding part of the good life.

Now bathrooms tend to be bigger. They tend to be compartmentalized for multiple uses. And many are geared for relaxation as well as efficiency. The whirlpool tub—a trimmed-down version of the outdoor spa—has become a focal point in many designs. The "master suite"—a formal integration of bedroom, bath, and auxiliary spaces—is perhaps the crowning expression of the bathroom's newly expanded identity. Exercise equipment, saunas, steam showers, grooming alcoves, walk-in dressing wings, even indoor atriums are all options in the new master suite.

As with contemporary kitchen design, there's a freer mixing of materials and styles; an emphasis on artificial lighting and an appreciation of natural light expressed in the use of windows, skylights, and glass block; an interest in raised ceilings and fine detailing; and a new creativity in approaches to cabinetry.

Antique fixtures and fittings are being treated with fresh respect, but teamed with a huge assortment of new styles and finishes.

There's a growing attention to water conservation—in fact, it's mandated in some communities. Manufacturers are offering ultra-low-flush toilets, low-flow shower heads, and sink faucets that save water or shut off when the user's hand is withdrawn.

Safety is a concern. It's now much easier to find sturdy grab bars, nonskid fixtures, and shatterproof materials. You can buy pressure-balancing or temperature-limiting plumbing fittings to prevent scalds.

As the population ages and we gain new awareness of the needs of the physically challenged, the "universal" or barrier-free bath is receiving deserved attention. Besides providing easy access, a major goal for today's barrier-free bath is aesthetic: it shouldn't look like a barrier-free bath.

Brainstorming a new bathroom is a threefold process—planning the space, defining a style, and choosing components. That's the sequence this book follows. You can tackle these steps in order or browse at will, either using the book as a detailed planning resource or simply choosing images and ideas to help your architect or designer understand more clearly what you want.

Ready to begin transforming that old bath? Simply turn the page.

A PLANNING PRIMER

Warm and traditional, high-tech, or colorfully whimsical: the individual styles may look different, but successful bathrooms have a lot in common. When a bathroom looks great and functions well, you can be sure that hours of planning went into its realization. Behind those shiny new fixtures and tiles are codes and clearances, critical dimensions, and effective design principles. Use this chapter as a workbook for basic planning. We help you evaluate your existing bathroom first. Then we guide you through layout and design basics, and finish up by explaining how design and construction professionals can help you. For inspiration, peruse the photos of successful bathrooms in the next two chapters. You'll see the latest in tubs and tiles, sinks and skylights, lighting and laminates. Soon you'll be on your way to creating the bathroom of your dreams.

a planning primer

taking
stock

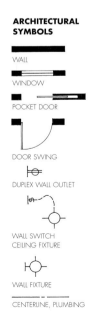

BEFORE YOU BEGIN *a bathroom shopping spree, take time to assess what you already have. A clear, accurate base map— such as the one shown below—is your best planning tool.*

Measure the space

To make your bathroom survey, you'll need either a folding wooden rule (shown above) or a steel measuring tape. First, sketch out your present layout (don't worry about scale), doodling in windows, doors, fixtures, and other features. Then measure each wall at counter height.

After you finish measuring, total the figures. Then take an overall measurement from corner to corner. The two figures should match. Measure each wall in the same manner.

Make a base map

Now draw your bathroom to scale on graph paper (most bathroom designers use ½-inch scale—¹⁄₂₄ actual size). An architect's scale is helpful but not really necessary. A T-square and triangle are all you need—plus some standard drafting paper with ¼-inch squares.

The example shown below includes a center-line to the sink plumbing and electrical symbols— for outlets, switches, and fixtures. Sketch in other features that might affect your plans.

A SAMPLE BASE MAP

**ARCHITECTURAL
SYMBOLS**

WALL

WINDOW

POCKET DOOR

DOOR SWING

DUPLEX WALL OUTLET

WALL SWITCH
CEILING FIXTURE

WALL FIXTURE

CENTERLINE, PLUMBING

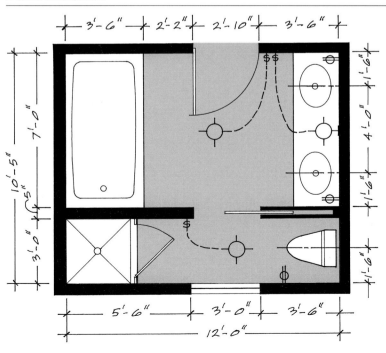

A Bathroom Questionnaire

This questionnaire can help you analyze conditions in your present bathroom as you begin to think about remodeling or adding another bath. When used with your base map, it also provides a good starting point for discussing your ideas with architects, designers, or showroom personnel. Note your answers on a separate sheet of paper, adding any important preferences or dislikes that come to mind. Then gather your notes, any clippings you've collected, and a copy of your base map, and you're ready to begin.

1. What's your main reason for changing your bathroom?

2. How many people will be using the room? List adults, children, and their ages.

3. Are users left-handed? Right-handed? How tall is each one?

4. Is the bath to be used by an elderly or disabled person? Is that individual confined to a wheelchair?

5. How many other bathrooms do you have?

6. Are you planning any structural changes?
   - ☐ Addition to existing house
   - ☐ Greenhouse window or sunroom
   - ☐ Skylight ☐ Other

7. Is the bath located on the first or second floor? Is there a full basement, crawl space, or concrete slab beneath it? Is there a second floor, attic, or open ceiling above it?

8. If necessary, can present doors and windows be relocated?

9. What's the rating of your electrical service?

10. What type of heating system do you have? Does any ducting run through a bathroom wall?

11. What is the style of your home's exterior?

12. What style (for example, high-tech, country, romantic) would you like for your new bathroom?

13. Do you favor compartmentalized layouts or a more open look?

14. List your present fixtures. What new fixtures are you planning?
    - ☐ Bathtub ☐ Shower ☐ Tub/shower combination
    - ☐ Vanity ☐ Sink or multiple sinks ☐ Toilet
    - ☐ Bidet

15. What secondary activity areas would you like to include?
    - ☐ Dressing area ☐ Makeup area
    - ☐ Steam shower or sauna ☐ Exercise facilities
    - ☐ Desk ☐ Entertainment center ☐ Garden
    - ☐ Laundry facilities

16. What color combinations do you like? And what fixture finish do you prefer: white, pastel, full color?

17. What cabinet material do you prefer: wood, laminate, or other? If wood, should it be painted or stained? Light or dark? If natural, do you want oak, maple, pine, cherry?

18. What countertop and backsplash materials do you prefer?
    - ☐ Laminate ☐ Ceramic tile ☐ Solid surface
    - ☐ Wood ☐ Stone ☐ Other

19. What are your storage requirements?
    - ☐ Medicine cabinet ☐ Drawers ☐ Vanity
    - ☐ Tall cabinet
    - ☐ Linen closet ☐ Laundry hamper or chute
    - ☐ Rollout baskets
    - ☐ Open shelving ☐ Other

20. What flooring do you have? Do you need new flooring?
    - ☐ Wood ☐ Resilient ☐ Ceramic tile ☐ Stone
    - ☐ Other

21. What are present wall and ceiling coverings? What wall treatments do you like?
    - ☐ Paint ☐ Wallpaper ☐ Washable vinyl paper
    - ☐ Wood ☐ Faux finish ☐ Ceramic tile ☐ Other

22. Would you prefer natural or mechanical ventilation?

23. What natural light sources are possible?
    - ☐ Skylight ☐ Window ☐ Clerestory
    - ☐ Glass block

24. Which forms of artificial lighting will you want?
    - ☐ Incandescent ☐ Fluorescent ☐ Halogen
    - ☐ 120-volt or low-voltage?

25. What lighting fixture types will you need?
    - ☐ Recessed downlights ☐ Track lights
    - ☐ Wall-mounted fixtures ☐ Ceiling-mounted fixtures
    - ☐ Makeup lights ☐ Indirect soffit lighting
    - ☐ Display lighting

26. What time framework do you have for completion?

27. What budget figure do you have in mind?

layout
basics

NOW COMES *the fun of planning your new bathroom. Layout is a three-part process that includes weighing basic options; blocking out placement of fixtures, cabinets, and amenities; and double-checking efficient heights and clearances. There's no perfect sequence—the trick is to work back and forth. These rules are not absolute, and in very small or oddly shaped spaces you'll certainly need to compromise.*

Classic layouts

While brainstorming, it helps to have some basic layout schemes in mind. The floor plans shown on the facing page are both practical and efficient. Keep in mind that these layouts can be combined, adapted, and expanded to meet your needs. For installation examples, see "Great Bathroom Ideas," beginning on page 27.

POWDER ROOM. This two-fixture room, also known as a guest bath or a half-bath, contains a toilet and a sink and perhaps some limited storage space. Fixtures can be placed side by side or on opposite walls, depending on the shape of the room. Very small sinks are available for extra-tight spaces.

Because the guest bath has high visibility but only sporadic use, it's a good place to enjoy more decorative but perhaps less practical finishes such as copper, glass, or upholstery. The door should swing open against a wall clear of any fixtures. Since space may be tight, a pocket door may be the solution.

Consideration should be given to privacy, ventilation, and soundproofing. A powder room should preferably open off a hallway—not off a living, family, or dining space.

FAMILY BATH. The family bath usually contains three fixtures—a toilet, a sink, and a bathtub or shower or combination tub/shower. The fixture arrangement varies, depending on the size and shape of the room. Family baths often have cluster, or corridor, layouts; these should be at least 5 by 7 feet.

Compartmentalizing fixture areas enables several family members to use the bathroom at the same time. A common arrangement is to isolate the toilet and shower (often including a small secondary sink in this area) from the basin and grooming area. This configuration can work well when adding a new bathroom isn't feasible.

The family bath is one of the most frequently used rooms in the house. Therefore, you'll want to choose durable, easy-to-clean fixtures and finishes.

CHILDREN'S BATH. Ideally, this bathroom is located so that each child has easy access.

When several children are involved, consider a single bath with two doors, or shared bathing and toilet facilities and an individual sink and

SAMPLE LAYOUTS

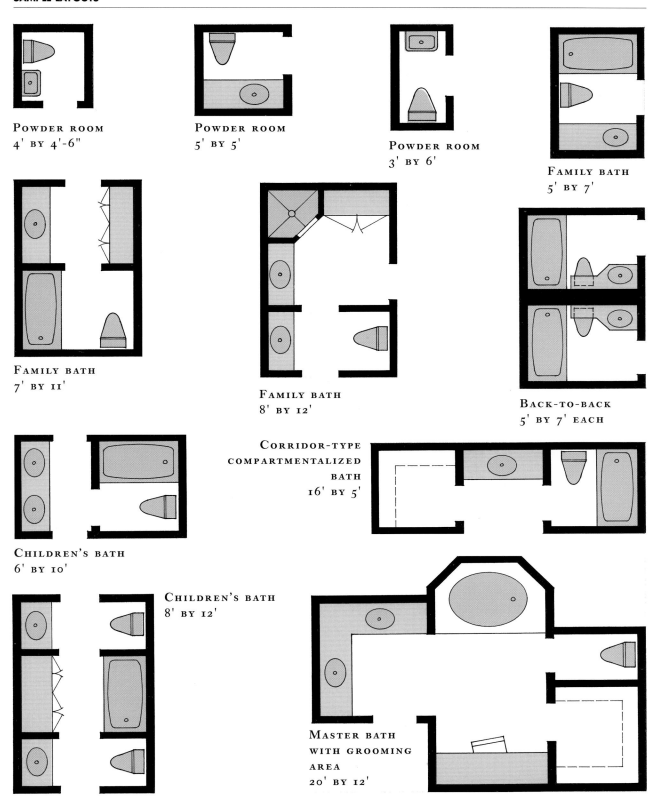

POWDER ROOM
4' BY 4'-6"

POWDER ROOM
5' BY 5'

POWDER ROOM
3' BY 6'

FAMILY BATH
5' BY 7'

FAMILY BATH
7' BY 11'

FAMILY BATH
8' BY 12'

BACK-TO-BACK
5' BY 7' EACH

CHILDREN'S BATH
6' BY 10'

CHILDREN'S BATH
8' BY 12'

CORRIDOR-TYPE
COMPARTMENTALIZED
BATH
16' BY 5'

MASTER BATH
WITH GROOMING
AREA
20' BY 12'

a planning primer

UNIVERSAL DESIGN

If you are remodeling a bath for a disabled or elderly person, or if you're simply looking down the road, be aware of the growing trend toward "universal" or barrier-free design.

Special heights, clearances, and room dimensions may be required. For instance, to accommodate a wheelchair, the room's openings—from door to shower to toilet enclosure—should be at least 34 inches wide. You'll also need to plan turnaround areas near fixtures; a 5-foot diameter is ideal. The door should swing out to allow easy movement in and out of the room. The shower should be curbless so a wheelchair can roll in unobstructed.

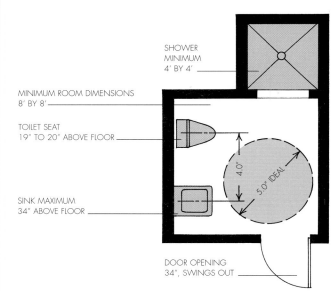

SHOWER
MINIMUM
4' BY 4'

MINIMUM ROOM DIMENSIONS
8' BY 8'

TOILET SEAT
19" TO 20" ABOVE FLOOR

SINK MAXIMUM
34" ABOVE FLOOR

4.0'

5.0' IDEAL

DOOR OPENING
34", SWINGS OUT

User-friendly heights are also critical. A sink must be no more than 34 inches from the floor and important storage areas should be between 15 and 48 inches high. It's important to leave an open space below the sink that allows ample knee room for a seated user; plan to cover under-sink plumbing. No handles, switches, or other controls should be more than 48 inches off the floor.

Exchange standard doorknobs, faucet handles, and cabinet hardware for levers and pulls that can be operated with one closed hand or a wrist. Grab bars are a boon in shower, tub, and toilet areas. Plan a seat inside the shower or tub. Extra lighting may also be required.

dressing area for each child. Color coding of drawers, towel hooks, and other storage areas can prevent territorial squabbles.

Children's baths require special attention to safety and maintenance. Single-control faucets minimize the possibility of a hot-water burn. Slip-resistant surfaces can help avoid accidents. Plastic-laminate counters and cabinets are durable and simplest to clean.

MASTER BATH/SUITE. This room has become more than just a place to grab a quick shower and run a comb through your hair. No longer merely a utilitarian space, today's master bath reflects the personality and interests of its owners. Besides toilet and bathing facilities and dressing and grooming areas, it can include amenities such as fireplaces, whirlpool baths, oversize tubs, saunas, and bidets. Outside such a bath is a natural place for a spa, sunbathing deck, or private garden.

Here are some "extras" you can plan into your master bath. Make sure that you provide adequate ventilation to prevent water damage (from splashes and condensation) to delicate objects and equipment.

■ **EXERCISE ROOM.** Depending on space, you can set up everything from a space-efficient "ballet barre" to a fully equipped in-house gym.

■ **MAKEUP CENTER.** A well-lit area for makeup application and storage is an asset in almost any bath. The area could include an adjustable makeup mirror with magnification and its own light source (see page 108).

■ **ENTERTAINMENT CENTER.** Whether built in or housed in a freestanding furniture piece, entertainment amenities like a TV, VCR, and sound system can amplify a master suite's sense of luxury and relaxation.

■ **ART GALLERY.** You can showcase works of art or build craft pieces, such as handmade tiles or a stained-glass window, right into the design.

■ **GREENHOUSE.** Because of the high moisture and humidity level, plants often thrive in a bathroom. It's an ideal place to bring a touch of nature into the house.

Arranging fixtures

The more facts you have available, the easier it will be to work with your layouts. You'll keep costs down if you select a layout that uses the existing water supply, drain lines, and vent stack. If you're adding on to your house, try to locate the new bathroom near an existing bathroom or the kitchen. It's also more economical to arrange fixtures against one or two walls, eliminating the need for additional plumbing lines.

To begin, position the largest unit—the bathtub or shower—within the floor plan, allowing space for convenient access, for cleaning, and (if needed) for bathing a child.

Next, place the sink (or sinks). The most frequently used fixture in the bathroom, the sink should ideally be out of the traffic pattern. Allow ample room in front for reaching below the sink, and give plenty of elbow room at the sides.

Locate the toilet (and bidet, if you have one) away from the door; often the toilet is placed beside the tub or shower. A toilet and bidet should be positioned next to each other. Don't forget the swing radius for windows and doors.

There are standard minimum clearances in a well-planned bathroom (see "Heights and clearances," below). If an elderly or disabled person will use the space, you'll need to increase these clearances as much as possible (see "Universal Design," on the facing page).

To visualize possible layouts, first draw scale outlines of fixtures and cabinets you're considering, then photocopy these and cut them out. Move the cutouts around on a tracing of your base map. Then draw the shapes onto the plan.

Heights and clearances

Building codes and bath industry guidelines specify certain clearances between, beside, and in front of bathroom fixtures to allow adequate room for use, cleaning, and repair. To help in your initial planning, check the minimum clearances shown at right.

Generally, you can locate side-by-side fixtures closer together than fixtures positioned opposite

MINIMUM FIXTURE CLEARANCES

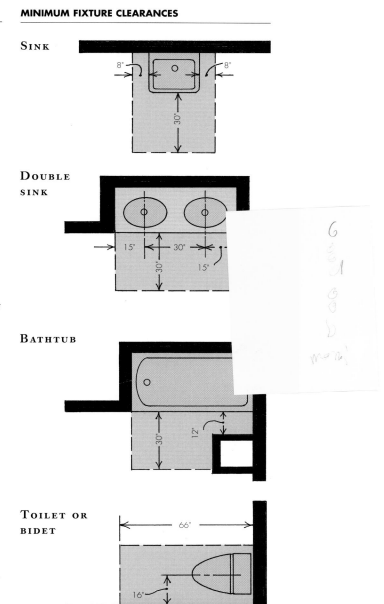

SINK

DOUBLE SINK

BATHTUB

TOILET OR BIDET

SHOWER

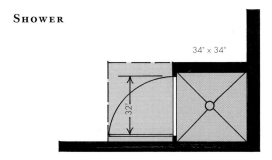

STANDARD HEIGHTS

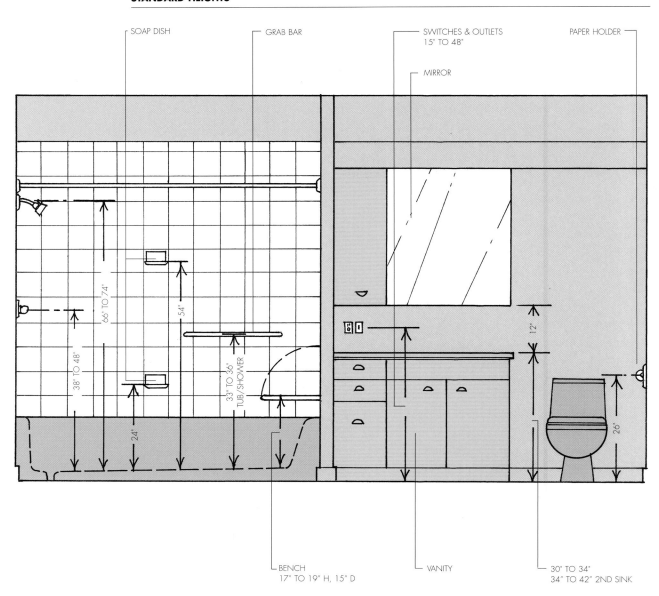

SOAP DISH   GRAB BAR   SWITCHES & OUTLETS   PAPER HOLDER
                                     15" TO 48"

MIRROR

66" TO 74"

54"

38" TO 48"

33" TO 36"
TUB/SHOWER

24"

12"

26"

BENCH   VANITY   30" TO 34"
17" TO 19" H, 15" D   34" TO 42" 2ND SINK

each other. If a sink is opposite a bathtub or toilet, keep a minimum of 30 inches between them, preferably more.

Shown above are standard heights for cabinets, countertops, shower heads, and accessories. If you're planning multiple sinks, the first should be no higher than 34 inches off the floor; if desired, the second may be between 34 and 42 inches above the floor, depending on the height of the user.

Playing it safe

About 25 percent of all home accidents occur in the bathroom. Through precautionary planning, however, you can greatly reduce the risk of injury.

First, select nonslip fixtures and surface materials. Anchor carpeting and buy rugs or bath mats with nonskid backing. Large tubs, especially those mounted in tall platforms or recessed with steps, are dangerous for children and adults with physical problems. Choose tempered glass, plastic, or other shatterproof materials for construction and accessories. Avoid mounting objects such as towel bars with sharp corners at eye level, and plan to clip or round countertop edges.

If children live in or visit your house, plan to store medicines and household cleansers in cabinets with safety latches or locks. Make sure that you can access the bathroom from the outside during an emergency.

Also be sure electrical receptacles are grounded and protected by ground fault circuit interrupters (GFCIs), which cut off power immediately if current begins leaking anywhere along the circuit. Outlets should be out of reach from the shower or bathtub. Keep portable heaters out of the bathroom. Install sufficient lighting, including a night light.

To avoid scalding, lower the setting on your water heater (see "Water and Energy Conservation," at right), install a temperature-limiting mixing valve, or use a pressure-balanced valve to avoid having sudden temperature drops.

Install L-shaped or horizontal grab bars, each capable of supporting 300 pounds, in tub and shower areas. Installation must be done properly—plywood reinforcing and bracing between wall studs may be required. Plaster-mounted bars don't provide reliable support.

What about storage?

While a powder room has minimal storage requirements, a family bath should include individual storage space for each family member, as well as places to keep cleaning supplies, paper products, soap, and incidentals. Vanities and other cabinets come with a variety of racks, shelves, pullouts, and lazy Susans, making limited storage space more efficient.

Today's bathrooms may also double as dressing and grooming areas as well; take time to consider these requirements. And how about a compact washer and dryer team, or a built-in ironing board?

WATER AND ENERGY CONSERVATION

There are several simple conservation measures you can take in the bathroom. If you intend to replace fixtures and fittings, look at those specifically designed to save water and energy. Many manufacturers offer water-saving toilets, faucets, shower heads, and hand-held shower attachments at prices comparable to those of their conventional counterparts. Such fixtures and fittings can reduce both the amount of water used and the amount of energy needed to heat water for bathing.

New ultra-low-flush (ULF) toilets use only 1.6 gallons or less per flush, compared with 5 to 7 gallons used by conventional toilets. These water-savers are often required in new construction. How much do ULFs really save over conventional toilets? Conservative estimates are 20 percent of total indoor water consumption for a family of four. Water-saving devices can be installed on old toilets.

GALLONS PER FLUSH

1½ GAL.   10,950

3½ GAL.   25,550

5 GAL.   36,500

GALLONS PER YEAR

New shower heads should be low-flow types, rated at no more than 2.5 gallons per minute. Some faucet and shower fittings include control devices that reduce flow while maintaining spray force. Others have aerators or fine mesh screens that break the water into droplets and disperse it over a wider area.

To save energy used for heating the bathroom and heating the water, make sure that the water heater, pipes, and walls are appropriately insulated. You can also save energy by reducing the water heater's temperature setting from the average 140°F to 110° or 120° (some older dishwashers, though, require water that's hotter).

For more details on water- and energy-saving products, see "A Shopper's Guide," beginning on page 79.

design ideas

WITH A *basic floor plan now in mind, you can begin to fine-tune your decorating scheme. Wall and ceiling coverings, flooring, woodwork, hardware, and even fixtures and fittings are powerful tools for evoking both style and mood. Style effects are directly linked to color, pattern, texture, size, and shape.*

You'll find scores of successful designs beginning on page 27. Here, we introduce some reliable design concepts—for you to use as starting points, not as strict rules.

What's your style?

A decorating style has physical characteristics that identify it with a particular region, era, or artistic movement—English Victorian, Southwestern, Arts and Crafts, Art Deco, and so on. Because certain colors, materials, and decorative motifs are linked to certain historic decorating styles, they can be used to evoke the character of a period—or simply to personalize and give dignity to a bland modern room.

Representative styles include the following:
- Period (or traditional)
- Regional
- Country
- Romantic
- Contemporary (also high-tech, modernistic)
- Eclectic

This said, rarely are styles slavish replicas of historical designs. More typically, designers select among elements that echo the mood of a particular period or look. What matters is that you choose a style and mood you find sympathetic and comfortable. And if the bathroom is linked to adjoining spaces, its look should match or at least complement the overall style.

Do you prefer quiet tradition or high-impact modernism? The elegant bath shown at left is dressed with classic stone surfaces, frame-and-panel cabinets, an arched window, and other traditional accessories. On the facing page, a bold, contemporary design continues step and square motifs found throughout the house; mirrored surfaces increase the impact.

Color or no color? The monochromatic, white-on-white scheme shown at right features artfully varied tile shapes and sizes for subtle visual interest. In contrast, the bath on the facing page playfully mixes warm red-stained woodwork, variegated pink concrete counter-tops, and yellow walls with cool-colored stone on floor and shower.

Line, shape, and scale

Three visual keys to planning a balanced, pleasing bathroom design are line, shape, and scale. You'll need to think about each of these elements—as well as color, texture, and pattern—to achieve the look you want.

LINE. Most bathrooms incorporate many different types of lines—vertical, horizontal, diagonal, curved, and angular. But often one predominates, and can characterize the design. Vertical lines give a sense of height, horizontals impart width, diagonals suggest movement, and curved and angular lines contribute a feeling of grace and dynamism.

Continuity of line unifies a design. Try an elevation (head-on) sketch of your proposed bathroom. How do the vertical lines created by the shower or tub unit, cabinets, vanity, windows, doors, and mirrors fit together? Does the horizontal line marking the top of the window align with those created by the tops of the shower surround, door, and mirror?

SHAPE. Continuity and compatibility in shape also contribute to a unified design. Of course, you needn't repeat the same shape throughout the room—carried too far, that becomes monotonous.

Study the shapes created by doorways, windows, countertops, fixtures, and other elements.

Look at patterns in your flooring, wall coverings, shower curtain, and towels. Are they different or similar? If similar, are they boringly repetitive? Think of ways to complement existing shapes or add compatible new ones; for example, you might echo an arch over a recessed bathtub in the shape of a doorway, or in shelf trim.

SCALE. When the scale of bathroom elements is in proportion to the overall size of the room, the design feels harmonious. A small bath seems even smaller if equipped with large fixtures and a large vanity. But the same bath can look larger or at least in scale if fitted with space-saving fixtures, a petite vanity, and open shelves.

Color

The size and orientation of your bathroom, your personal preferences, and the mood you want to create all affect color selection. Light colors reflect light, making walls appear to recede; thus, a small bath decorated in light colors feels more spacious. Dark colors absorb light and can make a ceiling seem lower or shorten a narrow room.

When considering colors for a small bathroom, remember that too much contrast has the same effect as dark color: it reduces the sense of expansiveness. Contrasting colors work well for adding accents or drawing attention to interesting structural elements. But if you need to conceal a problem feature, it's best to use one color throughout the area.

Depending on the orientation of your bathroom, you may want to use warm or cool colors to balance the quality of the light. While oranges, yellows, and colors with a red tone impart a feeling of warmth, they also contract space. Blues, greens, and colors with a blue tone make an area seem cooler—and larger.

A light, monochromatic color scheme (using different shades of one color) is restful and serene. Contrasting colors add vibrancy and excitement to a design. But a color scheme with contrasting colors can be overpowering unless you choose subdued tones of those colors.

Texture and pattern

Textures and patterns work like color in influencing a room's style and sense of space. The bathroom's surface materials may include many different textures—from glossy countertops to sturdy but soft-looking wood cabinets to rustically irregular terra-cotta tile flooring.

Rough textures absorb light, make colors look duller, and lend a feeling of informality. Smooth textures reflect light and tend to suggest elegance or modernity. Using similar textures helps unify a design and create a mood.

Pattern choices must harmonize with the predominant style of the room. Although we usually associate pattern with wall coverings or tile, even natural substances such as wood and stone create patterns.

While variety in texture and pattern adds interest, too much variety can be overstimulating. It's best to let a strong feature or dominant pattern be the focus of your design and choose other surfaces to complement rather than compete with it.

a planning primer

remodeling
realities

IF YOUR *bathroom needs only a new vanity, a faucet, and some wallpaper to update it, you probably won't need to find out just what lurks behind those walls. But if you're shifting or adding fixtures, installing a vent fan, or removing a wall, you'll have to bone up on some basic remodeling realities. These next pages offer an overview of bathroom systems.*

STRUCTURAL FRAMING

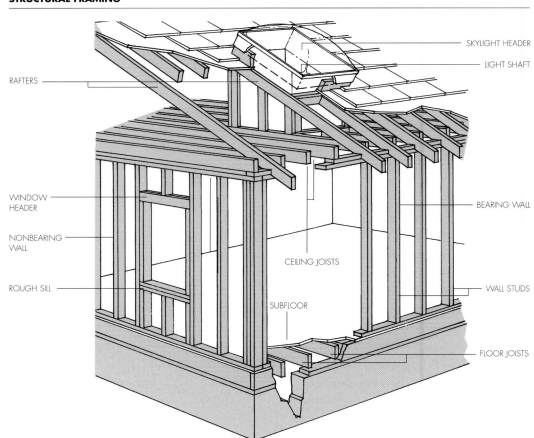

SKYLIGHT HEADER

LIGHT SHAFT

RAFTERS

WINDOW
HEADER

BEARING WALL

NONBEARING
WALL

CEILING JOISTS

ROUGH SILL

WALL STUDS

SUBFLOOR

FLOOR JOISTS

Structural changes

If you're planning to open up a space, add a skylight, or recess a shower or tub into the floor, your remodel may require some structural modifications.

As shown on the facing page, walls are either bearing (supporting the weight of ceiling joists and/or second-story walls) or nonbearing. If you're removing all or part of a bearing wall, you must bridge the gap with a sturdy beam and posts. Nonbearing (also called partition) walls can usually be removed without too much trouble—unless pipes or wires run through them.

Doors and windows require special framing, as shown; the size of the header depends on the width of the opening and your local building codes. Skylights require similar cuts through ceiling joists and/or rafters.

A standard doorway may not be large enough to accommodate a new tub or whirlpool. If you're remodeling, make sure you can get such a fixture into the room.

Hardwood, ceramic, or stone floors require very stiff underlayment. You may need to beef up the floor joists and/or add additional plywood or backerboard on top. For a large new tub, you may also need to supply stronger floor framing.

Plumbing restrictions

Your plumbing system is composed of two parts: a water-supply system, which brings water to the house and distributes it, and a drain-waste-ventilation (DWV) system, which removes water and waste.

Every house has a main soil stack. Below the level of the fixtures, it's the primary drainpipe. At its upper end, which protrudes through the roof, the stack becomes a vent. To minimize costs and keep the work simple, arrange a fixture or group of fixtures so they are as close to the present pipes as possible.

A proposed fixture located within a few feet of the main stack usually can be vented directly by the stack. Sometimes a fixture located far from the main stack requires its own branch

PLUMBING

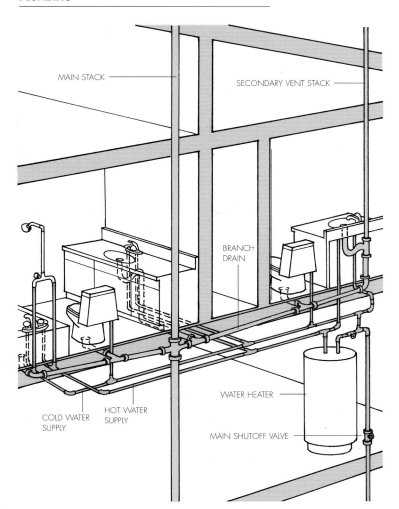

MAIN STACK

SECONDARY VENT STACK

BRANCH DRAIN

WATER HEATER

COLD WATER SUPPLY

HOT WATER SUPPLY

MAIN SHUTOFF VALVE

drain and a secondary vent stack (a big job). Be sure to check your local plumbing codes for exact requirements.

Generally, it's an easy matter—at least conceptually—to extend existing water-supply pipes to a new sink or tub. But if you're working on a concrete slab foundation, you'll need to drill through the slab or bring the pipes through the wall from another point above floor level.

Electrical requirements

When planning your new bathroom, take a good look at the existing electrical system. Most houses today have both 120-volt and 240-volt capabilities. But older homes with two-wire (120 volts only) service of less than 100 amps might not be able to supply the electricity needed to operate a new whirlpool tub, sauna, steam generator, or electric heater. You may need to upgrade your electrical system.

The National Electrical Code (NEC) requires that all bathroom receptacles be protected by ground fault circuit interrupters (GFCIs). If you're adding a new wall, you may be required by code to add an outlet every 12 feet or one per wall. In addition, codes may strictly dictate the placement of outlets, appliance switches, and even light fixtures in wet areas.

While it's possible to locate electrical wiring inside conduit that is surface-mounted, it is preferable to enclose all wires within the walls. Before completing your plan, try to track down any plumbing pipes, heating ducts, or other electrical wires already concealed there; sleuth from open areas (the basement, the attic, an unfinished garage) to identify spots where such utilities enter the walls.

ELECTRICAL WIRING

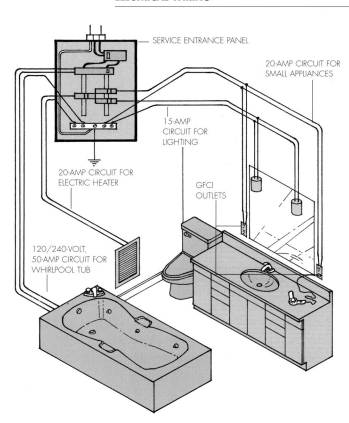

MECHANICAL SYSTEMS

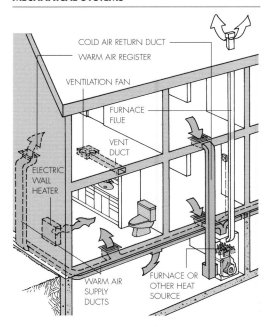

Mechanical (HVAC) systems

Unless the bath contains a heating duct and register, you'll need to determine how to extend the supply and return air ducts (a major undertaking) to connect with the rest of your central system. Since you'll be using the bathroom only intermittently, you may wish to provide an auxiliary heat source rather than link to your central system. A small wall- or ceiling-mounted heater can provide all the warmth you need. If you're working on an addition, consider installing a radiant-heat floor.

All gas heaters require a gas-supply line and must be vented to the outside, so you'll probably want to locate a gas heater on an exterior wall. Otherwise, you'll have to run the vent through the attic or crawl space and the roof.

Ventilation is critical. Even if you have good natural ventilation, you may want to add some forced ventilation. In a windowless bathroom, a fan is required by code. It's important that your exhaust fan have adequate capacity, rated in cubic feet per minute (CFM). The fan should be capable of exchanging the air at least eight times per hour. (For vent fan particulars, see page 99.)

DOLLARS AND CENTS

How much will your new bathroom cost? According to the National Kitchen & Bath Association, the average figure is $9,300. This is, of course, only the sketchiest of estimates. You may simply need to replace a countertop, add light fixtures, or exchange a worn-out bathtub to achieve a satisfying change. On the other hand, extensive structural changes coupled with ultra-high-end materials and fixtures can easily add up to $40,000 or more.

As shown below, labor typically eats up 21 percent of the pie; cabinets come in at around 33 percent; and, on the average, fixtures and fittings represent another 16 percent. Structural, plumbing, and electrical changes all affect the final figure significantly.

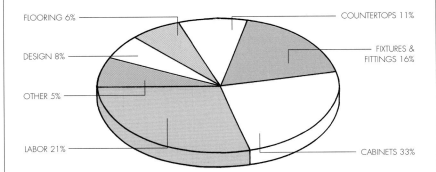

FLOORING 6%
DESIGN 8%
OTHER 5%
LABOR 21%
COUNTERTOPS 11%
FIXTURES & FITTINGS 16%
CABINETS 33%

How do you keep the budget under control? For starters, identify whether you're looking at a simple face-lift, a more extensive replacement, or a major structural remodel. Fixture, fitting, and material prices vary greatly. Obtain ballpark figures in different categories, mull them over, then present your architect, designer, or retailer with a range of options and a bottom line with which you can be comfortable. You can, of course, save a substantial piece of the pie by providing labor yourself—but be sure you're up to the task.

If you use a design professional, expect to be charged either a flat fee or a percentage (usually 10 to 15 percent) of the total cost of goods purchased. General contractors include the fee in their bids.

Don't make price your only criterion for selection. Quality of work, reliability, rapport, and on-time performance are also important. Ask professionals for the names and telephone numbers of recent clients. Call several and ask them how happy they were with the process and the results. Some may allow you to come and take a look at the finished work.

gearing up

ONCE YOU'VE *worked out an efficient layout, decided on storage requirements, and planned color and design schemes, it's time to draw up a revised floor plan. For help choosing new fixtures, cabinets, countertops, flooring, and so on, see "A Shopper's Guide," beginning on page 79. Be sure also to think about light fixtures and electrical switches and receptacles. And don't forget such finishing touches as doorknobs and drawer pulls, towel bars and moldings, curtains and blinds—details that can really pull a design together.*

The final plan

Draw your new floor plan, or working drawing, the same way you did the existing plan (see page 8). On the new plan, include existing features you want to preserve and all the changes you want to make. If you prefer, you can hire a designer, drafter, or contractor to draw the final plan for you. Elevation sketches usually aren't required, but they'll prove helpful in planning the work.

For more complicated projects, your local building department may require additional detailed drawings of structural, plumbing, and wiring changes. You may also need to show areas adjacent to the bathroom so officials can determine how the project will affect the rest of your house. To discover just which codes may affect your project and whether a permit is required, check with your city or county building department.

If you do the ordering of materials for your project, you'll need to compile a detailed master list. Not only will this launch your work, but it will also help you keep track of purchases and deliveries. For each item, specify the following information: name and model or serial number, manufacturer, source of material, date of order, expected delivery date, color, size or dimensions, quantity, price (including tax and delivery charge), and—where possible—a second choice.

Formal as can be, this bath includes lightly pickled frame-and-panel cabinets with crown moldings and furniture-like bases; elegant limestone on both floors and countertops; and a classic pewter finish on faucets, cabinet pulls, and wall sconces.

Need help?

The listing below covers professionals in bathroom design and construction and delineates some of the distinctions (although there's overlap) between architects, designers, contractors, and other specialists.

ARCHITECTS. Architects are state-licensed professionals with degrees in architecture. They're trained to create designs that are structurally sound, functional, and aesthetically pleasing. They know construction materials, can negotiate bids from contractors, and can supervise the actual work. Many architects are members of the American Institute of Architects (AIA). If structural calculations must be made, architects can make them; other professionals need state-licensed engineers to design structures and sign working drawings.

If your bathroom remodel involves major structural changes, an architect should be consulted. But some architects may not be as familiar with the latest in bathroom design and materials as other specialists.

BATHROOM DESIGNERS. These planners know the latest trends in bathroom fixtures and furnishings, but may lack the structural knowledge of the architect and the aesthetic skill of a good interior designer.

If you decide to work with a bathroom designer, look for a member of the National Kitchen & Bath Association (NKBA) or a Certified Bathroom Designer (CBD), a specialist certified by the NKBA. These associations have codes and sponsor continuing programs to inform members about the latest building materials and techniques.

INTERIOR DESIGNERS. Even if you're working with an architect or bathroom designer, you may wish to call on the services of an interior designer for finishing touches. These experts specialize in the decorating and furnishing of rooms and can offer fresh, innovative ideas and advice. And through their contacts, a homeowner has access to materials and products not available at the retail level.

Some interior designers offer complete remodeling services. Many belong to the American Society of Interior Designers (ASID), a professional organization.

GENERAL CONTRACTORS. Contractors specialize in construction, although some have design skills and experience as well. General contractors may do all the work themselves, or they may assume responsibility for hiring qualified subcontractors, ordering construction materials, and seeing that the job is completed according to contract. Contractors can also secure building permits and arrange for inspections as work progresses.

When choosing a contractor, ask architects, designers, and friends for recommendations. To compare bids, contact at least three state-licensed contractors. Give each bidder either an exact description of the proposed changes and a copy of your floor plan or plans and specifications prepared by an architect or designer. Be precise about who will be responsible for what work.

SUBCONTRACTORS. If you act as your own contractor, you will have to hire and supervise subcontractors for specialized jobs such as wiring, plumbing, and tiling. You'll be responsible for permits, insurance, and possibly even payroll taxes, as well as direct supervision of all the aspects of construction. Do you have the time and the knowledge required for the job? Be sure to assess your energy level realistically.

A traditional Japanese soaking tub is the focal point of this tile-lined open bath.

GREAT BATHROOM IDEAS

T HERE'S NOTHING LIKE a picture book when you're looking for inspiration. With this in mind, we offer the following gallery of bathroom designs. THE PHOTOGRAPHS included here represent as broad a range of styles as possible. You'll find small guest baths, larger family baths, and luxurious master baths. Some homeowners preferred restful, traditional rooms; others opted for open, contemporary expressions in glass and steel. All sought to make the space as pleasingly useful as possible. As one new master-suite owner commented, "All we need now is a hot plate." ONE OF THESE solutions may seem just right for your situation. Many of the approaches can be scaled up or down. Or you may simply wish to incorporate one or more of the design elements or fixture installations you see here into your own bath plan. In that case, consult "A Shopper's Guide," beginning on page 79.

great bathroom ideas

high
style

WE OPEN our pictorial showcase with an overview of bathroom looks and layouts. We present big rooms and small ones—powder rooms, family baths, children's baths, and luxurious master suites. Some of these projects were make-overs of existing rooms. Others borrowed space from adjoining rooms or pushed out into back gardens or side yards. A few were completely new additions or in new homes built from scratch. In your own planning, it's advisable to establish your space options early.

Do you want your bathroom strictly functional or outfitted with the latest amenities? The popular master suite is simply any large space that includes the bathroom, bedroom, and dressing room in one integrated layout. Satellite areas might house an exercise room, a whirlpool tub and sauna, a home office, a library, or a comfy couch and media center.

The two main poles of bathroom style are traditional and contemporary. Beyond that, there are period, regional, country, romantic, European-style, and eclectic looks. Hybrids abound. Many new designs strive to blend traditional looks with modern amenities such as whirlpool tubs and steam showers. As a starting point, do you want things streamlined or unfitted? High-tech or homey? Do you want one large area or separate compartments for different uses? You'll see all these approaches in the following pages.

Even a small bathroom can evoke a sense of serenity. This design in a tall, skinny space illustrates what you might call a luxurious minimalism, with industrial-looking plumbing fixtures and fittings providing their own spare form of ornament.

Wildly colorful tile brings a blast of fun to this shared children's space—and is easy to clean, too.

Exuding confident retro style, this formerly drab master bath is now splashed with intensely green Venetian-glass mosaic tiles. A walk-in, sealed steam shower (facing page) is the focal point; roomy, resin-coated wardrobe cabinets (upper left) and a credenza-style vanity lie beyond. These spaces gain light and some separation from the nearby bedroom through translucent wall panels (lower left) set behind the vanity's floating gilt mirror.

Glass block, a blue glass countertop, and white laminate Euro-style cabinets with stainless-steel detailing all contribute to a cleanly modern, minimalist look (right). Flooring is concrete with radiant heat. The cylindrical walk-in shower (top) features more curved glass block, with a strip in blue, plus carefully crafted tilework.

A tiny jewel, this small bath is the only one in the house, so every inch counts. The space-saving curved countertop (left) eases traffic flow and, along with the mirror's curved top, stretches the eye toward the tile-lined pedestal tub. A small built-in dressing bench (top) tucks into a corner between door and shower.

*A small single bath is
stretched by a clever
space-expanding trick:
the granite countertop
and cherry cabinets are
stylishly narrow except
where they bow out to
accommodate the
perfectly round sink.
Black diamond accent
tiles and the shower's
etched-glass door lend
an Art Nouveau air.*

A luxurious marble-lined whirlpool tub and walk-in shower (right) hold down one wall of this classic master-suite wing. Glass block and a skylight provide plenty of daylight while ensuring privacy. As the camera pans right, we walk through a door into the spacious dressing area (below), with floor-to ceiling storage cabinets on the left and a built-in makeup center at right. Beyond, through another door, lies a well-appointed exercise room, complete with its own auxiliary air-conditioning system.

This Asian-inspired master bath is in dressy black—from the rich slate of its floor, wainscoting, and walk-in corner shower to the glossy fixtures. Wall surfaces are hand-painted gilt for a soft but striking contrast.

Barrier-free baths can also be beautiful, as these two designs demonstrate. As shown at left, a marble-lined bathroom's accessible shower not only looks great but comes outfitted with an adjustable shower head, a padded bench, and a padded curb so the bather can ease right in. The design shown above uses a barrier-free pedestal sink, an angled mirror, and a cantilevered counter. Even the tub's grab bars and sinkside shower controls are good-looking.

Modern as can be, this guest bath's marble-trimmed walk-in shower (right) features a stainless-steel European-style "column" in its corner. In the opposite corner of the room, a techy steel pedestal sink (below) is reflected in floor-to-ceiling mirrors broken only by a vertical strip of makeup lights.

Here's another layout option: a free-floating vanity and makeup center that serves as a room divider (left). This partition wall, with cloudy lavender sponge paint making it seem to float upward from the limestone floor, conceals the bathing area. Turn the corner (below), and there are a curbless shower and pedestal-mounted tub wrapped with louvered windows.

In keeping with this home's Arts and Crafts styling, the bath is outfitted with a classic freestanding tub and twin pedestal sinks. White frame-and-panel wainscoting and window trim carry out the look, as do the period-style wall sconces. Marble floor tiles add a rich contrast.

This bathroom has a luxurious classicism. Arches spring from crisp white pilasters, and marble is everywhere—in muted beige on the walls and in multihued mosaic bands on the floor. The imposing, twin-basin console sink is topped by a gilt mirror; fittings and accessories are also coated in gold.

Why not dress a bathroom like any other room? In this unfitted traditional design, what looks like an antique country table is a new custom-built vanity with turned wooden legs and a limestone top scooped for double sinks. The fir-framed medicine cabinet is 6 inches deep—twice the standard size—to make up for losing covered storage underneath the sinks. Tiled wainscoting, a sisal rug, creamy wall sconces, and classic crown moldings round out the look.

Clean white woodwork, hand-painted tile, and subtle pink wallpaper distinguish this fastidiously detailed, romantic-style bath. Looking past the shower and one grooming area, you see the wood- and tile-lined pedestal tub and a garden view.

Every detail of this expanded master bath is richly inventive. A built-in, stair-stepped cabinet divides the bathroom from the bedroom beyond. Combining openness with privacy, the shower stall's interior glass wall is sandblasted to chest height. Sliding glass doors open to a deck, helping to dissolve the distinction between indoors and out.

Attic spaces are naturals for bathroom additions, but all those roof angles can present a puzzle. This small guest bath gains daylight from a custom angle-topped window. An old-fashioned claw-foot tub and freestanding vanity open up floor space, revealing more of the homey fir planks.

Wrapped in comfortable carpeting, this high-ceilinged master suite extends past twin vanities to the bath area beyond. The back-to-back sink areas are identical; they're separated by large grooming mirrors housed in clear glass frames, through which both light and views may enter. The marble-lined pedestal tub is backed by large greenhouse windows; the wall of a patio beyond protects the bather's privacy.

on the surface

MANY STYLES are established, at least in part, by the materials you choose for countertops, floor coverings, and wall and ceiling treatments. Also factor in the finishes on cabinets, fixtures, fittings, and accessories.

Just a few years ago, the average vanity top, usually laminate, included a 4-inch lip on the back. Today's higher backsplashes, however, often feature materials that are found there alone. Geometric or handpainted art tiles are popular choices. Seamless backsplash mirrors are popular, too—but can be tough to keep clean.

Floor choices are increasing. Besides time-tested tile and vinyl, we're seeing more stone used in baths—the result of newly affordable stone-tile offerings and the sealers that protect them. Wood and carpeting are also showing up, especially in detached areas away from direct-splash zones.

For painting walls, both standard treatments and faux finishes are familiar. Other wall options include tile, stone, terrazzo, wood, plaster, wallpaper, upholstery, and glass block.

Beyond aesthetic considerations, you should weigh the physical characteristics of surface materials. Most bathrooms take a lot of wear. Is your countertop choice water resistant, durable, and easy to maintain? Is the floor hard to walk on, noisy, or slippery? Are walls easy to clean? A powder room or master suite might be the place to try delicate materials that would be impractical in a family bath.

Guest baths are a place to try a new wall treatment. Here, colored joint compound was knife-applied over a lighter base tint; a top glaze accents both.

Intricate North African-derived tile designs fill both walls and floor, but somehow look all of a piece. The two dominant patterns, on walls and floor, are separated by contrasting borders.

This master bath, designed to coexist with existing bathrooms from the 1920s, is a striking example of balanced tile design. Floor diagonals of earthy quarry tile are echoed by diagonals on the countertops and backsplash; green trim tile fronts the cabinets. Matching Malibu designs are used on floor borders and backsplash, and the tub surround is marked by a complementary pattern.

A tropical fish peers imperturbably from the oceanic backdrop of a tubside wall. This custom work artfully blends both mural and mosaic techniques, as painted pieces follow natural contours instead of a rigid grid.

In this colorful bathing space, a stainless-steel soaking tub occupies an outside corner below windows with partially sandblasted glass panels. The nearby surfaces are clad with marble and slate tiles and terra-cotta-colored plaster.

Bright and cheery, this country bath carries white-painted beaded wainscoting along the walls, around the tub, and even inside the tubside display niche.

Stylishly traditional, this bathroom showcases formal frame-and-panel walls throughout. The sink area has classic wood frames surrounding the green marble panels, but in the adjacent shower area the panel framing switches subtly from painted wood to white, watertight marble.

Clean white woodwork and Carrara marble set the tone, but the unusual floor strikes a pleasingly contrasting note. The stained fir floor's central "rug" is made from bamboo; it's set off by a painted black inlay.

Here's a study in black, white, and chrome. The white is Carrara marble. Cabinets are black lacquer below and, flanking the mirror, stainless steel with frosted-glass door panels. Walls and ceiling are coated with rough-textured plaster—in a water-proof formulation designed to survive humid spaces.

Wallpaper, whether used overall, above wainscoting, or simply for an ornate border, is showing new flair. This powder room wears a hand-painted, hand-embossed pattern.

Don't rule out upholstery: its benefits include elegant color, soft texture, and good soundproofing. The upholstered walls shown here create a romantic-style backdrop for a makeup center.

Textured-looking faux-finished walls, baseboards, and ceiling trim form a visual partnership with the freestanding vanity's carved front. A hand-painted concrete floor completes the picture.

Stone-textured concrete tiles are wrapped in square-within-square fashion by contrasting concrete rectangles and small square accents. The glass-tile baseboard shows just how well mosaic tiles can handle curves.

waterworks

Y OUR CHOICES of sink, tub, and shower do a lot to determine how your bathroom will be used, the way its traffic will flow, and what its general ambience will be like. In the following pages, we honor these often unsung heroes. You'll find more on fixtures in "A Shopper's Guide," beginning on page 79.

Sink designs have become wildly varied in the last few years. You'll see both pedestal and wall-hung sinks, in a rainbow of colors and finishes and in classic, retro, and contemporary styles. Both deck-mounted and integral sinks are sporting new looks. And what about a sculptural sinktop basin? Faucets and fittings also come in many new shapes and finishes.

Tubs form another focal point—a symbol of luxury and repose. You can choose a basic bathtub or a classic, freestanding claw-foot model. Pedestal tubs present a seamless, built-in look to the world. Whirlpool tubs abound. Or consider a traditional soaking tub in acrylic or wood.

Tub/shower units save space, but if the room is available, most users prefer to have a separate shower. Though market offerings include a plethora of prefabricated stalls, the larger, custom walk-in shower—perhaps with a built-in bench—is worth a careful look. Or examine the sleek new European modules, some with multiple shower heads, computerized temperature controls, even built-in audio systems. You'll find myriad options in shower fittings. When planning a shower, remember to think about ventilation, lighting, and privacy.

Like an art installation, this elegant terra-cotta sink and its freestanding, hand pump-inspired faucet give washing your hands a theatrical quality.

Try to find the faucet downspout: it's hidden under the raised section of the stainless-steel counter behind the integral sink. Only the faucet handles—minimalist curves of steel—are visible.

A *crystal sink bowl sits atop a transparent shelf in a small powder room. Drain fittings run through the glass countertop, making a design statement of their own.*

An elliptical console sink with sculptural legs strikes a traditional tone in this bathroom. It's stylistically at home with classic tile work on the walls and floor.

Gracefully blending the old and the new, a modern whirlpool tub meets turn-of-the-century wood wainscoting and marble; chrome accessories glow with soft filtered light from etched-glass windows.

A combination of a Japanese-style soaking tub and a modern shower, this granite-surfaced fixture runs the full width of a narrow bathroom wall. The over-scaled window adds light and visually stretches the space while allowing bathers to contemplate the land-scape beyond.

A wooden soaking tub sits atop a command-ing corner pedestal, surrounded by curved marble steps and counters. The floor is mosaic tile, and walls gleam with alternating bands and patches of wall tile and trim. The tub is centered below an airy skylight well.

Like a futuristic monolith, this striking cylindrical shower "pod" is the sculptural heart of an ultramodern master bath. For privacy's sake in the multiuse room, the shower's lower sections are translucent rather than transparent.

Pale green glass mosaic tiles line a spacious tub/shower corner, complete with Roman tub spout, whirlpool jets, hand-held shower, and standard wall-mounted shower head. An operable porthole window provides light and ventilation.

great bathroom ideas

bright ideas

A GOOD LIGHTING PLAN provides shadowless, glare-free illumination for the entire bath as well as bright, uniform light for specific tasks. And as you'll see, openings and light fixtures can also create dramatic visual effects.

Daylight can enter a bathroom through windows, skylights, doors, or all three. When a bathroom faces the street or the neighbors, it may be best to trade a little light for privacy. Glass block, translucent glazing, and decorative glass—stained, sandblasted, or beveled—all can provide decorative flair while maintaining a reserved exterior.

Besides natural light, you'll need good artificial lighting. The trick is to provide task light that's gently flattering and yet strong enough for grooming (for details, see pages 106–107). Be sure to choose warm fluorescent tubes or bulbs with good color-rendering properties for accurate makeup light and reliable skin tones.

A lone, low-voltage pendant with a beaded-glass shade is reflected in the sinkside mirror. The mirror also shows a black track fixture that lights the bath space beyond.

Black tiles drink up lots of light, but this room's glazing is up to the balancing act. Steel-framed windows back both the sink area and a short return wall; they're met by glass block, which follows the sinuous curves of the tub while yielding both light and privacy. A small awning window opens off the tub for ventilation.

Other use areas such as the tub, shower, and toilet compartments, may need their own light fixtures. Fluorescent sources can give good general lighting, and are required in some energy-conscious areas. Indirect fixtures work well: consider cove lighting, soffit lighting, translucent diffusers, and other bounce sources that spread a soft, even light.

Multiple sources and multiple controls allow you to alternate between morning efficiency and nighttime repose. Consider dimmers here. Also plan to provide low-energy night lighting for safety and convenience.

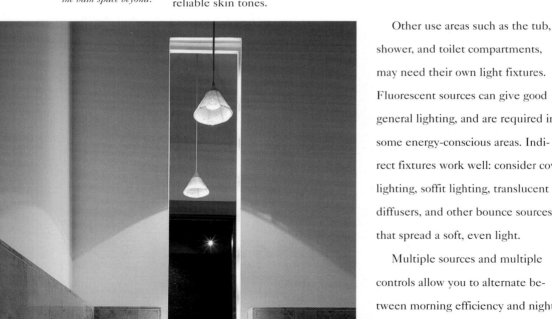

A rustic bathroom's hinged wooden windows surround a granite-wrapped pedestal tub, opening the room directly to the deck and landscape beyond.

Like a lovely green wind, these elegant stained-glass windows atmospherically enhance a luxurious pedestal tub. The leaded glass makes a bright focal point while ensuring privacy.

This bath opened right onto a neighbor's view, so the architect used some nontraditional glazing in the sinkside window frames. Most of the lower "window" sections are mirrored; besides aiding grooming, they reflect light and views from another source. The sculptural ripple inserts do admit light, but their translucent nature masks views in and out.

This master bath's task light comes from a diffused inset fixture (shown at left) that puts makeup light right where it's needed. Additional ambient light glows from a translucent panel housed in the display niche; its source is a bank of fluorescent tubes concealed in a storage cabinet beyond. Continuing the subtle illumination scheme, the shower (above) has a panel in its ceiling that evenly diffuses light from a bright tungsten fixture.

Small baths can gain a semblance of extra space with window pop-outs. In this case, the shower/tub area has been stretched with a greenhouse window unit, which adds daylight, views, display space, and—thanks to its translucent, tempered wall panels—a measure of seclusion.

This comfortable master bath has a long, open fir vanity with a
hand-tooled marble top. The corresponding mirror-faced cabinet is
broken by flush-mounted incandescent vertical tubes for makeup light,
and the backsplash and counter areas are washed by additional light
from beneath the cabinet. A double-hung wooden window further
brightens the room.

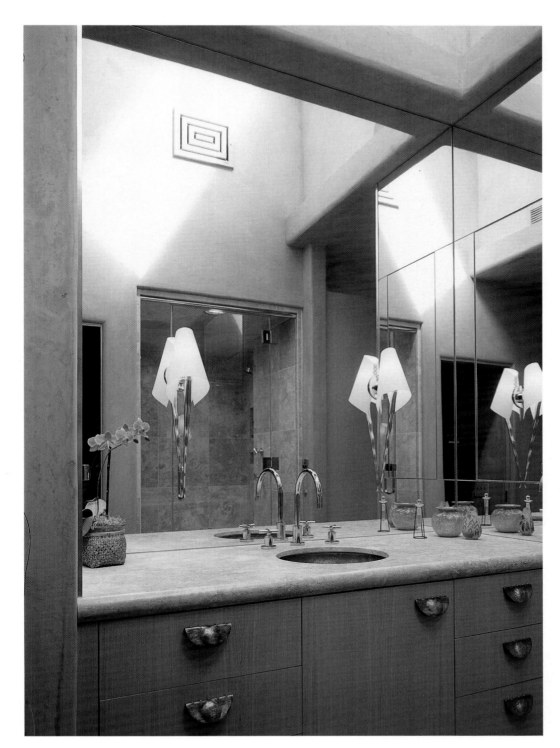

At either side of the sink, stylish wall sconces are mounted directly to the seamless mirrored surface, giving the area balanced, effective grooming light. A skylight well above brings welcome daylight to the windowless space.

great bathroom ideas

elegant options

As LIFE speeds up, many of us treasure our quiet time. So it's understandable that for some people the bathroom is becoming a down-time retreat including such extras as a soaking tub, exercise area, and comfortable sitting space. Even such standard living-room features as fireplaces, media centers, wet bars, and art displays are moving in. Master suites blur the distinctions between bed and bath, organizing separate zones for bathing, grooming, dressing, working, and relaxing in a private part of the house. The desire for repose may tempt you to provide a comfortable couch, built-in bookcases, and perhaps a corner wet bar or espresso counter. Maybe you'd like built-in audio speakers connected to a central home system (it's a good idea to have at least a separate volume control in the bathroom). Or indulge yourself in a large-screen TV or full-blown home theater serving both bed and bath areas.

Situated just off the main bath, this dressing room uses pine built-ins and a cushion-topped dressing bench to frame a decorative leaded-glass window.

The view from tubside shows two additional wings in a classic master-suite layout. At back left, a fitness room is equipped with an exercise bike, a treadmill, a dumbbell set, and a wall-mounted TV. At back right, a grooming center fits alongside a built-in dresser; a walk-in dressing room lies just beyond.

If you'd like a traditional dressing table, you'll need to find a spot for it out of the main flow. Where will you store cosmetics, jewelry, and accessories? What mirrors and lighting will you need? Do you want an auxiliary sink?

A walk-in closet can neatly com-bine clothes storage with a dressing area. Or opt for built-in drawers, pullouts, and a freestanding closet or armoire. If space permits, this area can serve as a bridge between bed-room and bath. Good ventilation, especially for areas adjacent to a shower or tub, is crucial.

*A comfortable
bedroom, a cheery
two-sided fireplace,
and a whirlpool tub
all team up in this
spacious master suite.
The bath continues
around the corner.
Elegant granite and
cozy carpeting help tie
the areas together.*

*When it's windy, cold, and dark out-
side, what could be more relaxing
than slipping into a warm tub
and taking a long soak in front
of a blazing fire? This bathroom
revolves around a 5- by 8-foot
platform with a whirlpool bath;
the two-way fireplace sits in a wall
shared by the adjacent bedroom.*

A cedar-and-granite grooming area (above), complete with twin sinks and expansive mirrors, occupies one wall of a comfortable master suite. A striking cedar storage wall (right) divides bedroom from bath and also works, on the bedroom side, as a headboard.

As today's bath serves more functions, it may incorporate traditional closet and bureau units. This dressing room links a master bedroom with the bath proper and features maple built-ins with lots of nooks and crannies. There's also a comfortable shoelace-tying sitting spot.

This white laminate built-in presents a seamless European-style face of flush-front doors and drawers; mirrors add space-stretching flash to an otherwise blank wall.

A tiled sink counter steps down smoothly to a cushy, built-in window seat, perfect for a quiet, private read. Leaded-glass windows behind supply lots of natural light.

This bedroom/bath transition zone combines
an antique vanity and a large framed mirror to create a stylish makeup area. The
window bay beyond, trimmed with
traditional frame-and-panel woodwork,
becomes a light-filled sitting spot.

A SHOPPER'S GUIDE

NOT TOO long ago, you simply purchased a white pedestal sink, a mirrored medicine cabinet, a 30- by 60-inch tub, and a toilet and called it a bathroom. But much has changed. Today, there are integral solid-surface sinks; contoured acrylic whirlpool tubs; one-piece, ultra-low-flush toilets. And that's just the beginning of what's new. Who has the time and energy to sort it all out? **THIS CHAPTER** will help. Our color photographs present the latest in fixtures and materials. And text and comparison charts give you the working knowledge to brave the showrooms, to communicate with an architect or designer, or simply to replace that dingy, old-fashioned wall covering with something both more stylish and more practical. **ARMED WITH THE BASICS**, it's much easier to go on to the fine points. Most bathroom professionals are knowledgeable and ready to assist. Often you can borrow literature, samples, and swatches to bring home to check for color, size, and stylistic compatibility.

Cabinets

STYLISH STORAGE BOXES HELP SET THE TONE

In earlier days, "bathroom storage" meant a clunky medicine cabinet mounted above the pedestal or wall-hung lavatory sink. Then along came boxy vanities, and the bathroom acquired a bank of drawers to one side of the plumbing compartment.

As changing life-styles demand expression and bathrooms become grooming centers, exercise gyms, and spas, storage needs and configurations are also changing. One or more base cabinets may still form the backbone of the contemporary storage scheme, but bath storage areas have become more stylish, their design integrated with that of mirrors, sink, lighting, and backsplash treatments. Perhaps you'll wish to curve a custom unit around a corner, let built-ins form knee walls between use areas, or plan a floor-to-ceiling storage column.

Traditional or European-style?

First, you'll need to choose between two basic cabinet styles, frame and frameless.

Traditional American cabinets mask the raw front edges of each box with a 1-by-2 "faceframe." Doors and drawers then fit in one of three ways: flush; partially offset, with a lip; or completely overlaying the frame. The outer edges of the faceframe can be planed and shaped (called "scribing") to fit the contours of an adjacent wall or ceiling. But the frame takes up space and reduces the size of the openings,

CABINET CLOSE-UPS

FACEFRAME CONSTRUCTION

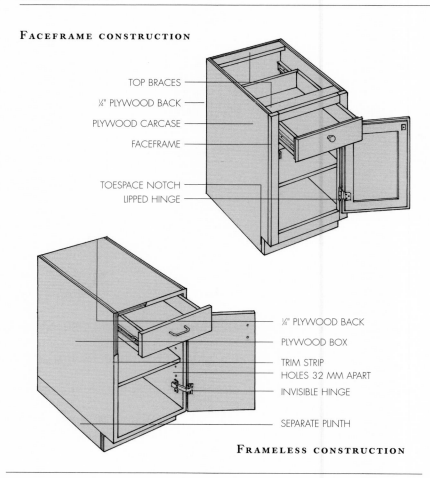

TOP BRACES
¼" PLYWOOD BACK
PLYWOOD CARCASE
FACEFRAME

TOESPACE NOTCH
LIPPED HINGE

¼" PLYWOOD BACK
PLYWOOD BOX
TRIM STRIP
HOLES 32 MM APART
INVISIBLE HINGE
SEPARATE PLINTH

FRAMELESS CONSTRUCTION

so drawers or slide-out accessories must be significantly smaller than the full width of the cabinet.

Europeans, when faced with post-war lumber shortages, came up with "frameless" cabinets. A simple trim strip covers raw edges, which butt directly against one another. Doors and drawers often fit to within ⅛ inch of each other, revealing a thin sliver of the trim. Interior components—such

as drawers—can be sized larger, practically to the full dimensions of the box.

The terms "system 32" and "32-millimeter" refer to precise columns of holes drilled on the inside faces of many frameless cabinets. These holes are generally in the same place no matter what cabinets you buy, and interchangeable components such as shelf pins and pullout bins just fit right into them.

Bathroom cabinets are sporting
new looks—and some old ones,
too. The styles
shown here include a furniture-
like, frame-and-panel
piece with built-in valance
lighting (above); a space-saving
corner pedestal in traditional
cherry (left); and a
modern update of the tried-
and-true medicine cabinet that
includes strip lights and other
amenities (right).

Stock, custom, or modular?

Cabinets are manufactured and sold in three different ways. The type you choose may affect the cost, appearance, and workability of your bathroom.

STOCK CABINETS. Mass-produced, standard-size cabinets are the least expensive option, and they can be an excellent choice if you clearly understand what cabinetry you need. You may find stock lines heavily discounted at some home centers. A recent development, the so-called RTA ("ready-to-assemble") cabinet, costs even less but requires some basic tools and elbow grease to put together. An RTA vanity is shown on the facing page.

As the name implies, the range of stock sizes is limited. Even so, you can always specify door styles, direction of door swing, and finish of side panels.

CUSTOM CABINETS. Many people still have a cabinetmaker come to their house and measure, then return to the cabinet shop and build custom cabinet boxes, drawers, and doors.

Custom shops can match old cabinets, size oddball configurations, and accommodate complexities that can't be handled with stock or modular units. But such work can cost considerably more than medium-line stock or modular cabinets.

MODULAR SYSTEMS. Between stock and custom cabinetry are "custom modular cabinets" or "custom systems," which can sometimes offer the best of both worlds. They are manufactured, but they are of a higher grade and offer more design flexibility than stock cabinets. Not surprisingly, they cost more, too.

A CORNUCOPIA OF CABINET PULLS

You can change virtually everything on these basic modules: add sliding shelves; replace doors with drawers; add wire bins, hampers, and pullouts. If necessary, heights, widths, and depths can be modified to fit almost any design. Be advised, though: these cabinets could take a long time to show up at your doorstep.

READY-TO-ASSEMBLE (RTA) CABINET

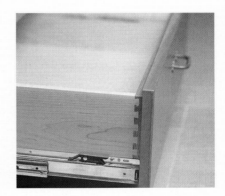

What about dimensions?

The classic bathroom vanity measured about 32 inches high (with countertop) by 21 inches deep and about 30 inches wide. But bath cabinets are growing—new offerings may be up to 36 inches high by 24 inches deep and 48 inches wide. You can make longer cabinet runs by joining units together.

Some bath cabinet lines include wall cabinets and tall storage units; otherwise, look to kitchen cabinet manufacturers for ideas.

Judging quality

Within each line, costs are largely determined by the style of the doors and drawers you choose. The simplest, least expensive option is often a flat or "slab" door, popular for seamless European designs. Frame-and-panel designs are more traditional and come in many versions, including raised panel (both real and false), arched panel, beaded panel, and recessed or flat panel.

To determine the quality of a cabinet, first look closely at the drawers. They take more of a beating than any other part of your cabinets. Several drawer designs are shown at far right. You'll pay a premium for such features as solid-wood drawer boxes, sturdy dovetail joints, and full-extension, ball-bearing guides.

Are cabinet pulls included? If not, you'll pay more for them, but you'll be able to choose exactly what you want. For a sampling, see the photo on the facing page.

Door hinges are critical hardware elements. European or "invisible" hinges are most trouble-free; consider these unless you need the period look of surface hardware. Check for adjustability; hinges should be able to be reset with the cabinets in place.

Most cabinet boxes are made from sheet products like plywood, particleboard (plain or laminated), or medium-density fiberboard. Though solid lumber is sometimes used, it is usually saved for doors and drawers.

Hardwood plywood is surfaced with attractive wood veneers on both face and back. The higher the face grade, the more you'll pay. Particleboard costs less, weighs more, and is both weaker and more prone to warping and moisture damage than plywood. Generally, particleboard vanities are faced with high-pressure plastic laminate or with a softer material called melamine. Medium-density fiberboard (MDF), a denser, furniture-grade particleboard, is available with high-quality hardwood veneers.

Be sure to examine drawer components and hardware. Options shown here, top to bottom, include budget-oriented melamine drawer boxes with self-closing epoxy guides; sturdy, full-extension, ball-bearing guides; and premium hardwood boxes with dovetail joints and invisible, under-mounted guides.

Countertops

MODERN ALTERNATIVES FOR CLASSIC SURFACES

Even after being steamed or splashed, good countertops still come up shining because they're moisture resistant—or better yet, waterproof. The best materials look great under stress and are less likely to scratch or chip.

What are your choices?

Plastic laminate, ceramic tile, solid-surface acrylics, and stone are the four major countertop materials in current use. Synthetic marble, while still common, is losing some ground to solid-surface materials. Custom glass and cast concrete are gaining in popularity, especially in stylish master suites and powder rooms. Wood is sometimes used for countertops, too; but to prevent water damage, the surface of wood countertops must be treated (perhaps repeatedly) with a durable finish.

Shopping around

When shopping, you probably won't be able to compare all the materials in one place. Some dealers with showrooms are listed in the yellow pages under Countertops or Kitchen Cabinets & Equipment; they'll probably have tile, plastic laminate, solid-surface products, and—maybe—wood. Large building-supply centers carry plastic laminate, synthetic marble, and

---

COMPARING COUNTERTOPS

Plastic laminate

Advantages. You can choose from a wide range of colors, textures, and patterns. Laminate is durable, easy to clean, water resistant, and relatively inexpensive. Ready-made molded versions are called postformed; custom or self-rimmed countertops are built from scratch atop particleboard or plywood substrates. There are many laminates available for these tops, and edging options abound. With the right tools, you can install laminate yourself.

Disadvantages. It can scratch, chip, and stain, and it's hard to repair. Ready-made postformed tops can look cheap, and other edgings may collect water and grime. Conventional laminate has a dark backing that shows at its seams; new solid-color laminates, designed to avoid this, are somewhat brittle and more expensive. High-gloss laminates show every smudge.

Ceramic tile

Advantages. It's good-looking; comes in many colors, textures, and patterns; and is heat resistant and water resistant if installed correctly. Cost runs from inexpensive to pricey, depending on whether the tile is formed by machine or by hand and how many units are needed. Buy a tile that's rated for countertop use. Grout is also available in numerous colors. Patient do-it-yourselfers are likely to have good results.

Disadvantages. Some tile glazes can react adversely to acids or cleaning chemicals; be sure to ask. Many people find it hard to keep grout satisfactorily clean. Using epoxy grouts and thin, uniform grout lines can help. The hard, irregular surface can chip china and glassware.

wood. For other dealers or fabricators, check the categories Marble—Natural; Plastics; Glass—Plate; Concrete Products; and Tile. Designers and architects can also supply samples.

Backsplash fever

These days, bathroom designers are using the backsplash— the wall surface surrounding the countertop proper—to make an aesthetic statement.

A good backsplash also has practical advantages: if properly installed, it seals the area from moisture, and it makes the wall a lot easier to clean.

COMPARING COUNTERTOPS

Solid-surface

Advantages. Durable, water resistant, heat resistant, nonporous, and easy to clean, this marble-like material can be shaped and joined with virtually invisible seams. Different edge treatments are available. It allows for a variety of sink installations, including integral units that combine both basin and countertop (see page 86). Blemishes and scratches can be sanded out.

Disadvantages. It's expensive, requiring professional fabrication and installation for best results. It needs very firm support below. Until recently, color selection was limited to white, beige, and almond; now stone patterns and pastels are common. Costs climb quickly for wood inlays and other fancy edge details.

Synthetic marble

Advantages. This group of man-made products, collectively known as "cast polymers," includes cultured marble, cultured onyx, and cultured granite. All three are relatively easy to clean. Cultured onyx is more translucent than cultured marble. These products are often sold with an integral sink. Prices range from inexpensive to moderate. You can color-coordinate a synthetic marble top with tub, shower, and wall panels.

Disadvantages. Synthetic marble is not very durable, and scratches and dings are hard to mend (the surface finish is usually only a thin veneer). Backings, typically, are porous. Quality varies widely; look for Cultured Marble Institute or IAPMO certification.

Stone

Advantages. Granite, marble, and limestone, all popular for countertops, are beautiful natural materials. In most areas, you'll find a great selection of colors and figures. Stone is water resistant, heatproof, and very durable. Surface finishes range from polished to honed (matte) and even rougher textures. A number of thicknesses are available, and edges can be shaped in numerous ways.

Disadvantages. Oil, alcohol, and any acid (even chemicals in some water supplies) can stain marble or limestone and damage its finish; granite can stand up to all of these. Solid slabs are very expensive. Some designers suggest stone tiles—including slate—as less expensive choices. When shopping, take time to study the latest sealer options.

Sinks and Faucets

WASHING UP IN STYLE—ANY STYLE

No longer just a basin and a mirror, the sink area has become a thoughtfully planned environment for grooming and personal care. Layouts with two sinks—housed in one continuous vanity, in side-by-side alcoves, or in matching configurations on opposite walls—are popular. Some bathrooms also include a separate, smaller wash basin in the toilet compartment or makeup area.

Sinks and faucets have become design accents in their own right—a comparatively low-commitment way to try adding a bit of dash to an otherwise restrained design scheme. (If you later decide you don't like the boldness, it's a lot simpler to change a faucet than a shower or tub surround.)

Sink options, new and old

Sinks are available in a huge array of styles, shapes, and materials. You can make the sink stand out—or blend its look with that of a period-style tub, shower, or toilet fixture. Whether for an antique or ultramodern design, some sink manufacturers can provide custom colors on special orders.

DECK-MOUNTED SINKS. The vanity-bound basin is still the most common arrangement. You'll find a wide selection of materials in deck mounts, including vitreous china, fiberglass-reinforced plastic, enameled steel, and enameled cast iron. Vitreous china (made with clay that's poured into molds, fired in a kiln, and glazed) is heavy, comes in many colors, and is easy to clean; it also resists scratches, chips, and stains. Fiberglass is lightweight and moderately priced, but tends to scratch and dull. An enameled steel surface is easy to clean and lighter and less expensive than vitreous china or enameled cast iron—but also much less durable. Enameled cast iron is more expensive and durable than vitreous china or enameled steel, but is very heavy.

Other sink materials include translucent glass, hand-painted ceramics, stainless steel, brass, copper, and even wood. These materials are strikingly elegant as accents but can require zealous maintenance.

You have a choice of mounting methods with various deck-mounted models. Self-rimming sinks with molded overlaps are supported by the edge of the countertop cutout; flush deck-mounted sinks have surrounding metal strips to hold the basin to the countertop; unrimmed sinks are recessed under the countertop and held in place by metal clips. Some deck-mounted sinks are designed as seemingly "free-standing" fixtures, where the entire basin sits sculpturally atop the counter and drains down through it.

INTEGRAL-BOWL SINKS. A solid-surface countertop (see page 85) can be coupled with a molded, integral sink for a sleek, sculpted look. The one-piece molded unit sits on top of a vanity or cabinet; predrilled holes are often part of the package. A countertop with an integral bowl has no joints, so installation and cleaning are easy.

Sink color can either match the countertop or complement it; for example, you might choose a cream-colored sink below a granite-patterned counter. Edge-banding and other border options abound. Other integral sinks come in cast polymers, vitreous china, and fiberglass.

Check the sink's depth before buying: some versions may be shallower than you'd like.

PEDESTAL SINKS. Pedestal sinks are making a big comeback, in a wide range of traditional and modern

New sink models include a wide range of both deck-mounted designs and above-counter versions. You'll also find a growing number of eclectic, almost sculptural sinks, like the one shown below right.

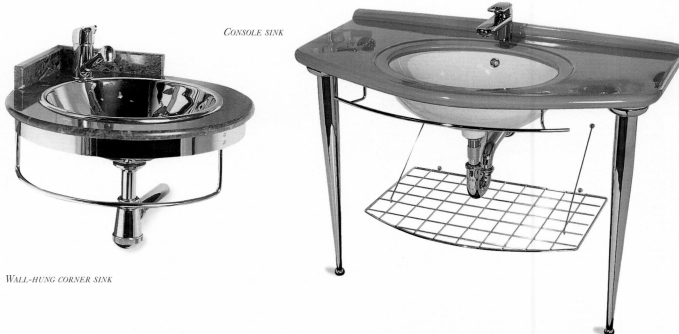

CONSOLE SINK

WALL-HUNG CORNER SINK

PEDESTAL SINKS

designs. Typically of vitreous china, these elegant towers are usually easy to install and clean around. The pedestal often, but not always, hides the plumbing.

Pedestal sinks are typically among the highest-priced basins. Another disadvantage: they provide no storage space below the basin.

WALL-HUNG SINKS. Like pedestals, wall-hung sinks are enjoying a contemporary revival. Materials and styling are along the same lines; in fact, some designs are available in either version.

Wall-hung sinks come with hangers or angle brackets for support. Generally speaking, they are among the least expensive and most compact sink options and are relatively easy to install. If you're putting in a wall-hung model for the first time, plan to tear out a strip of the wall to add a support ledger.

CONSOLE SINKS. If you like the look of pedestal or wall sinks, but yearn for a bit more elbow room, take a look at so-called console sinks. These "stretch models" join a wider rectangular deck with either two or four furniture-like vanity legs. Some versions include storage space below.

Faucets

The world of sink faucets is constantly changing, presenting new colors, shapes, styles, and accessories.

Popular finishes include polished chrome, brushed chrome, nickel, polished or antiqued brass, soft pewter, elegant gold plate, and jazzy enameled epoxy. For durability and low maintenance, polished chrome with a high nickel content is still the best bet. You can choose a showstopper in boldest modern or most quaintly antique styling, coordinate with tub fittings, or pick the same handles for all fixtures in the room.

You can buy faucets with digital temperature readouts, scaldproof models, and spouts that stop the flow when your hand is removed. How about a swiveling European faucet with an adjustable spray, a drinking spout, and a gum-massage attachment?

Sink faucets are available with single, center-set, or spread-fit controls. A single-control fitting has a combined faucet and lever or knob controlling water flow and temperature. A center-set control has separate hot and cold water controls and a faucet, all mounted on a base or escutcheon. A spread-fit control has separate hot and cold water controls and an independently mounted faucet. Pop-up or plug stoppers are sold separately or with the faucet and water controls.

When you're attracted to clever, streamlined designs, ask yourself two questions. How well could you work the controls with soaped-up hands and sleep-bleared eyes? And how easy would it be to clean or maintain the installation?

Whatever style you choose, most bathroom professionals agree that you get what you pay for. Solid-brass workings, though pricey, are considered most durable. Ceramic-disk and plastic-disk valve designs are generally easier to maintain than older washer schemes.

While most faucets are sink-mounted, other installations call for either deck-mounted or wall-mounted fittings. When you select your sink, be sure any holes in it will match the type of faucet you plan to buy, as well as any additional accessories.

Sink faucets run the gamut from antiquelike to high-tech, from soft pewter-finish to jazzy epoxy, and from single-control to spread-fit.

Tubs and Showers

LUXURIOUS OPTIONS FOR QUIET SOAKS, BOLD SPRAYS

In many modern baths, the tub is the focus of the room, a gratifying symbol of luxury and relaxation. In new installations, whirlpool tubs—now available in more traditional tub styles and sizes—are in high demand.

But for on-the-go workday bathing, a separate shower, unless space prohibits, is a nearly universal request. A well-designed shower is also safer to use than many tub/showers, which may lack both firm footing and adequate grab bars.

Tub choices

The market overflows with bathtub styles. The 30- by 60-inch tub, which often controlled the dimensions of the 5- by 7-foot bathroom of the past, no longer rules the buyer. Tubs come in new and more com-

MOLDED WHIRLPOOL TUB

fortable shapes and sizes and in a wide range of styles and colors.

THE BASIC BATHTUB. The boxy, familiar tub is enameled steel, relatively inexpensive, and lightweight—

but noisy, cold, and prone to chipping. Built-to-last enameled cast-iron tubs are more durable and warmer to the touch, but very heavy (they may require structural reinforcement).

Traditional tubs come in two basic styles: recessed and corner. Recessed tubs fit between two side walls and against a back wall; they have a finished front or "apron." Corner models have one finished side and end and may be right- or left-handed. Some more stylish tubs are finished on three sides, allowing placement along an open wall.

A 72-inch-long tub is better than the standard 60-inch model, if space allows; a depth of 16 inches is more comfortable than the standard 14.

CLAW-FOOT TUB

PEDESTAL TUB

hot-water connection; once your soak is over, the water is drained.

Most models resemble standard acrylic platform tubs; a pump and venturi jets are what create the whirlpool effect. Jet designs vary. Generally, you can opt for high pressure and low volume (a few strong jets) or low pressure and high volume (lots of softer jets). Typically, the more jets, the easier it is to access an aching body part—though some users find these setups less soothing and prefer the massage effect of the stronger jets.

Though some professionals build custom whirlpool tubs from scratch and even retrofit old bathtubs, it's simplest and safest to buy a complete whirlpool kit. Look for a unit that's UL-approved. Want extras? Consider adding a digital temperature control, a timer, a built-in fill spout, or a cushy neck roll.

THE AGE OF PLASTICS. The most innovative tubs these days are usually plastic—either vacuum-formed acrylic or injection-molded thermoplastics like ABS. These lightweight shells are easy to transport and retain heat well. But best of all is their range of contours and sizes. Plastic tubs are available in neutrals and in the latest colors. The one drawback: dark, shiny surfaces tend to scratch or dull easily.

These tubs are usually designed for platform or sunken installation. Some models sit atop the surrounding deck, like a self-rimmed sink; others are undermounted. Though warmer to the touch than cast iron, plastic tubs lack iron's structural integrity—be sure to provide solid support beneath one.

FREESTANDING TUBS. An old-fashioned freestanding tub, such as the enduring claw-foot model, makes a nice focal point for a traditional or country design. You can buy either new reproductions or a reconditioned original. Such tubs can double as showers with the addition of Victorian-inspired shower-head/diverter/curtain rod hardware.

Looking for traditional fixtures and fittings? Recently, many new sources for renovators' supplies have sprung up; check specialty shops and antique plumbing catalogs.

WHIRLPOOL TUBS. Think of these hydromassage units simply as bathtubs with air jets. Unlike an outdoor spa, the whirlpool uses a standard

SOAKING TUB

CURBLESS BUILT-IN SHOWER

laminate, and synthetic marble. Some have ceilings. For comfort, choose a shower that's at least 36 inches square.

The term "shower stall" needn't mean something boxy and boring—or even, for that matter, economical. Circular, corner, and angular wraparounds are available with enough spray heads and accessories to please the most demanding shower connoisseur. Circular showers often have clear or tinted acrylic doors that double as walls.

BUILD YOUR OWN. You can also mix and match base, surround, and doors to create the shower of your choice.

A shower base or "pan" can be purchased separately or in a kit that includes the shower surround. Most bases are made of plastic, terrazzo (a concrete/stone mix), cast polymer, or solid-surface materials and come in standard sizes in rectangular, square, or corner configurations with a predrilled

Because of their extra weight when filled, deep whirlpool tubs may need special floor framing. Your unit may also require a dedicated 120- or 240-volt circuit to power the pump and controls.

SOAKING TUBS. These tubs, like Japanese furos (made of wood), have deep interiors. They come in recessed, platform, and corner models, with rectangular or round interiors of fiberglass or acrylic.

Hot tubs, which use a wooden-barrel design and continuous water supply, can present moisture problems in all but the best-ventilated spaces. They are probably best confined to a deck or private garden.

Shower styles

You can select a prefabricated shower stall, match separate manufactured components, or build completely from scratch. Think about amenities such as a comfortable bench or fold-down seat, adjustable or hand-held shower heads, a place for shampoos and shaving equipment, and sturdy grab bars.

PREFABRICATED SHOWER STALLS. If your remodel calls for moving walls or doors, you may be able to fit a one-piece molded shower or tub/shower surround through the opening—though these units are really designed for new houses or additions. One-piece showers are available in fiberglass-reinforced plastic, plastic

PREFABRICATED CORNER SHOWER

hole for the drain. It's easy to find a base that works with another maker's tub since many manufacturers produce both—and in many colors. Of course, you can also have a tile professional float a traditional mortar base and line it with the tile of your choice.

Shower surrounds require solid framing for support. You can add prefabricated wall panels or use a custom wall treatment such as ceramic tile, stone, or a solid-surface material over a waterproof backing. Molded wall panels of fiberglass or synthetic marble may include integral soap dishes, ledges, grab bars, and other accessories. These manufactured panels are sized for easy transport, then assembled and seamed on-site.

Doors for showers come in a variety of styles: swinging, sliding, folding, and pivoting. For tub/showers, choose sliding or folding doors. Doors and enclosures are commonly made of tempered safety glass with aluminum frames. These frames come in many finishes; you can select one to match your fittings. The glazing itself can be clear, hammered, pebbled, tinted, or striped. The seamless look is popular, though expensive.

Swinging, folding, and pivoting doors can be installed with right or left openings. Folding doors are constructed of rigid plastic panels or flexible plastic sheeting. Glass requires more maintenance; some bathers keep a squeegee nearby for daily cleaning.

Multitier cedar benches (right) help turn a space into a comfortable, burn-free sauna room. Trim wall controls (top) drive a built-in steam shower.

SAUNAS AND STEAM SHOWERS

These luxurious features, once found mainly in gyms and health clubs, have recently been invited to enter the residential bathroom as well.

A sauna is a small wood-lined room (often sold prefabricated) that heats itself to around 200°F. Traditionally, sauna walls, ceilings, floor slats, and benches are built from wood such as aspen, redwood, or cedar. Besides insulated walls, a solid-core door, and double-paned glass (if any), you'll also need an electric or gas sauna heater, a thermostat and timer, some lighting, and both inlet and outlet vents for cross-ventilation. Minimum size for a sauna is about 65 cubic feet per person.

Steam hardware for residential use is compact enough to be housed in any number of locations—inside a storage cabinet, in an adjacent closet or alcove, or in a nearby crawl space. The generator is sized according to the number of cubic feet in your enclosure and, to a lesser extent, the material the enclosure is made from. Besides the steam box, outlets, and control pad, all you need is an airtight shower door, a comfortable bench, and a waterproof, steam-resistant surround. Your new shower may already meet these requirements.

Of course, people with known cardiovascular problems should be cautious about using a sauna or steam.

Tub and shower fittings

These days you'll find nearly as many styles and finishes for tub and shower fittings as for bathroom sinks. In addition, you can choose a line of integrated fittings, or at least use the same handles and finish from sink to tub to shower.

TUB FITTINGS. For tub/showers, you can opt for either single or separate controls. Tubs require a spout and drain. Tub/showers need a spout, shower head (see facing page), diverter valve, and drain. These can be deck- or wall-mounted; some installations use a combination. The best fittings have solid brass workings and come in many finishes, including chrome, brass, nickel, pewter, gold plate, and enameled epoxy. You'll also find color-coordinated pop-up drains and over-flow plates.

Ever had a tub spout poke you while you were trying to relax? Mount it along the back wall or deck. Position handles where you can get to them easily. Roman or waterfall spouts are striking-looking and can fill tubs much faster than standard fittings—assuming that supply pipes (see page 21) are large enough for the task.

Unfortunately, tubs, especially whirlpools, aren't great for really getting clean. For that, add a separate hand shower controlled by a nearby diverter valve.

SHOWER FITTINGS. Multiple, adjustable, and low-flow are the bywords for today's shower fittings. Large walk-in showers often have two or more shower heads: fixed heads at different levels, or hand units on adjustable vertical bars. Massage units and overhead "shampoo" heads often supplement the basic head or heads.

ROMAN TUB SPOUT

WALL SPOUT

DECK-MOUNT FITTINGS WITH HAND SHOWER

"SHAMPOO" SHOWER HEADS

TEMPERATURE-LIMITING VALVE

ADJUSTABLE BAR WITH HAND SHOWER

SPRAY-BAR JETS

"Surround" designs combine one or more fixed heads with wall-mounted auxiliary jets or adjustable multijet vertical bars. How do you control all these jets? Diverters may have three or more settings for orchestrating multiple water sources. It's smart to consult a bathroom professional for complex shower schemes—otherwise, you may experience unequal pressures and water temperatures.

Safety plays a part in new designs, too. If you've ever suffered a pressure drop when someone flushes a toilet or starts the washer, you'll appreciate single-control shower fittings with pressure balancing to prevent scalding rises in temperature. Several companies make designs that incorporate adjustable temperature limiters. You can also buy quick-reacting thermostatic valves, with or without zoomy digital readouts.

Low-flow shower heads, rated at 2.5 gallons per minute or less, are required in much new construction, and many cities are demanding that less efficient heads be replaced in bathroom remodels.

You'll probably find that low-flow retrofits splash more and are slightly noisier than standard heads. Less expensive models deliver fine droplets that won't wet your body as quickly—and might even feel a little cool by the time they get down to your knees. On/off valves are built into many low-flow heads. Make sure levers are shut-offs, not just spray adjustments.

For safety and convenience, it's best to place shower controls to the front and/or side of the enclosure—not directly below the shower head.

Toilets and Bidets

FRONT-PAGE NEWS ABOUT TWO HO-HUM FIXTURES

TRADITIONAL TWO-PIECE TOILET

Now styling, new colors, and new efficiency have all but replaced the tried-and-true water closet. In addition to standard and antique models, vitreous china toilets now come in sleek-looking European designs, standard or low-profile heights, and rounded or elongated bowls. Do you want classic white, shiny black, or a soft pastel? Ultra-low-flush or pressure-assisted mechanics?

The bidet is a European standby that's gaining popularity on this side of the Atlantic. It's used primarily for personal hygiene. Like toilets, bidets are made of vitreous china, in a number of styles, colors, and finishes to match toilets and other fixtures.

Toilets

As water shortages drive home the fact that water is a finite resource, the new word in toilets is ultra-low-flush (ULF). Why change? Older toilets use 5 to 7 gallons or more per flush. In 1994, codes were changed to require 1.6-gallon-per-flush toilets for new construction. Some water districts even offer a rebate if you install a ULF fixture in your present home.

Some homeowners complain that ultra-low-flush toilets don't really save water in the long run because they may require several flushings. One reply to this problem is the pressure-assisted design, which uses a strong air vacuum to power a quick, intensive flush. Pressure-assisted models are noisier than other low-flush toilets, but the disturbance is very brief.

The basic choice in toilets is between traditional two-piece and European-style one-piece designs. Two-piece toilets have a separate tank that's either bolted directly to the bowl or, in the case of some period reproductions, mounted on the wall above. One-piece toilets are also known as "low-boy" or "low-profile" models. Some toilets come with seats, some don't. If you're splurging, you might consider an electronic seat that's heated and/or programmed with a bidet-like spray jet.

Before installing a new toilet in an older house, check the offset—the distance between the back wall and the center of the drain hub (measured to the hold-down nuts). Most newer models are designed for a 12-inch offset.

How about retrofits? Variable-buoyancy flappers, flap actuators that ride on the overflow tube, and dual-handle mechanisms will greatly increase the efficiency of your existing water-guzzler. Some water districts will send you parts free. With the new devices, you still have the pressure of the original volume, but the flap will close while several gallons still remain in the tank.

Bidets

A bidet, best installed next to the toilet, is floor-mounted and plumbed with hot and cold water. Available in styles and finishes to match new toilets, it comes with either a horizontal spray mount or a vertical spray in the center of the bowl. Some models include rim jets to maintain bowl cleanliness. Most versions have a pop-up stopper that allows the unit to serve also as a footbath or laundry basin.

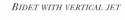

BIDET WITH VERTICAL JET

In the past, "ultra-low-flush" sometimes meant very little flush. A pressure-assisted toilet tank uses water-compressed air to add a power boost. It's noisier than some flushing actions, but just for a moment.

LOW-PROFILE, ONE-PIECE TOILET (LEFT) AND BIDET

Heating and Ventilation

CLEAR THE AIR WHILE TAKING THE CHILL OFF

Certain elements of your bathroom's climate—steam, excess heat, early morning chill—can be annoying and unpleasant. When you remodel, consider adding an exhaust fan to freshen the air and draw out mold-producing moisture and a heater to warm you on cool days. Installing such climate controllers may be simple, and could make a big difference.

Heating the bathroom

Nothing spoils the soothing effects of a long, hot soak or shower faster than stepping out into a cool room—or even one of average house temperature. A small auxiliary heater in the wall or ceiling may be just what you need to stay warm while toweling off. Add a timer, and you can wake up to a toasty bathing space.

Bathroom heaters warm rooms by either of two methods—convection or radiation. Convection heaters warm the air in a room; radiant heaters emit infrared or electromagnetic waves that warm objects and surfaces.

ELECTRIC HEATERS. Because electric heaters are easy to install and clean to operate, they're the most familiar choice. Besides the standard wall- and ceiling-mounted units, you'll find heaters combined with exhaust fans, lights, or both.

Wall- or ceiling-mounted convection heaters usually have an electrically heated resistance coil and a small fan to move the heated air. A toe-space heater—recessed into a vanity below the sink—helps warm (and dry) the floor more quickly. Options include thermostats, timer switches, and safety cutoffs.

Radiant heaters using infrared light bulbs ("heat lamps") can be surface-mounted on the ceiling or recessed between joists.

GAS HEATERS. You'll find heaters available for either propane or natural gas. Though most are convection heaters, there is one radiant type—a catalytic heater. Regardless of how they heat, all gas models require a gas supply line (see page 22) and must be vented to the outside.

HEATED TOWEL BARS. Besides gas and electricity, another heat source has reappeared on the bathroom scene: hot water. The original idea was to warm and dry bath towels, but now these hydronic units—wall- or floor-mounted—are being billed as "radiators" as well. In addition to water-powered towel warmers, you can also find sleek electric versions (see below right).

Ventilating the bathroom

Even if you have good natural ventilation, an exhaust fan can exchange the air in a bathroom faster, and in bad weather it can keep the elements out and still remove stale air. Some fans include lights or heaters or both.

It's important that your exhaust fan have adequate capacity. The Home Ventilating Institute (HVI) recommends that the fan be capable of exchanging the air at least eight times every hour. To determine the required fan capacity in cubic feet per minute (CFM) for a bathroom with an 8-foot ceiling, multiply the room's length and width in feet by 1.1. For example, if your bathroom is 6 by 9 feet, you would calculate the required fan capacity as follows:

6 x 9 x 1.1 = 59.4 CFM

Rounding off, you would need fan capacity of at least 60 CFM. If your fan must exhaust through a long duct or several elbows, you'll need greater capacity to overcome the increased resistance. Follow the manufacturer's recommendations.

Most fans have a noise rating measured in sones: the lower the number, the quieter the fan.

Heated towel bars keep bath linens toasty while doubling as radiators. Brass rack (facing page) harnesses old-fashioned hydronic heat; modern slat design (right) comes in many colors—and in both hydronic and electric versions.

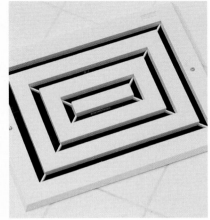

Most modern vents and heaters are trim, discreet built-ins. A ceiling fan (above right) blends with white field tiles and draws heat and moisture from shower steam. An electric toe-space heater (above left), centered below the sink area, emits welcome warmth on chilly mornings.

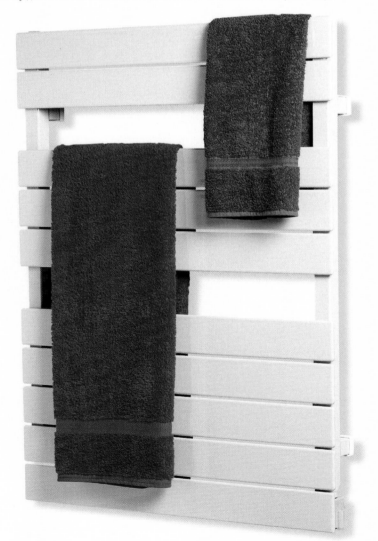

Flooring

HARD-WORKING FOUNDATIONS DANCE NEW STEPS

The primary requirements for a bathroom floor are moisture resistance and durability. Resilient tiles and sheets, ceramic tile, and properly sealed masonry or hardwood are all good candidates. Resilient flooring is the simplest (and usually the least expensive) to install; the others are a little trickier. For a touch of comfort, don't rule out carpeting, especially the newer stain-resistant industrial versions.

Planning checkpoints

Confused by the array of flooring types available? For help, study the guide below. It's a good idea to visit flooring suppliers and home centers. Most dealers are happy to give or lend samples to study.

For safety's sake, a bathroom floor must be slip resistant, especially in wet areas. Tiles, either ceramic or resilient, are safest in matte-finish or textured versions. Smaller ceramic tiles, with the increased number of grout surfaces they require, offer extra traction. A rubberized mat or throw rug (if it will stay put) can provide firm footing—and a warm landing zone—near the tub or shower.

Don't be afraid to mix and match flooring materials. Today's layouts often use different materials in the wet and dry areas of the bath. Cozy carpeting is showing up in dressing

---

COMPARING FLOORING

Resilient

Advantages. Generally made from solid vinyl or polyurethane, resilients are flexible, moisture and stain resistant, easy to install, and simple to maintain. Another advantage is the seemingly endless variety of colors, textures, patterns, and styles available. Tiles can be mixed to form custom patterns or provide color accents.

Sheets run up to 12 feet wide, eliminating the need for seaming in many bathrooms; tiles are generally 12 inches square. Vinyl and rubber are comfortable to walk

on. A polyurethane finish may eliminate the need for waxing. Prices are generally modest, but expect to pay a premium for custom tiles and imported products.
Disadvantages. Resilients are relatively soft, making them vulnerable to dents and tears; often, though, such damage can be repaired. Tiles may collect moisture between seams if improperly installed. Some vinyl still comes with a photographically applied pattern, but most is inlaid; the latter is more expensive but wears much better.

Ceramic tile

Advantages. Made from hard-fired slabs of clay, ceramic tile is available in hundreds of patterns, colors, shapes, and finishes. Its durability, easy upkeep, and attractiveness are definite advantages.

Tiles are usually classified as quarry tiles, commonly unglazed (unfinished) red-clay tiles that are rough and water resistant; terra-cotta, unglazed tiles in earth-tone shades; porcelain pavers, rugged tiles in stonelike shades and textures; and glazed floor tiles, available in glossy, matte, or textured finishes.

Floor tiles run the gamut of widths, lengths, and thicknesses—8-inch and 12-inch squares are most plentiful. Costs range from inexpensive to moderate; in general, porcelain is most expensive. Purer clays fired at higher temperature generally make costlier but better-wearing tiles.
Disadvantages. Tile can be cold, noisy, and, if glazed, slippery underfoot. Porous tiles will stain and harbor bacteria unless properly sealed. Grout spaces can be tough to keep clean, though mildew-resistant or epoxy grout definitely helps.

areas, grooming centers, and even exercise rooms. Hardwood strips or planks can play a similar role in period or country designs.

If you're on a tight budget, save the honed marble or fine ceramic tile for a focal point, such as around a platform tub or walk-in shower.

What about subflooring?

Don't make any final decision until you know what kind of subfloor your new flooring will require.

With proper preparation, a concrete slab can serve as a base for almost any type of flooring. Wood subfloors are not suitable for rigid materials such as

masonry and ceramic tile unless they are built up with extra underlayment or floor framing. But adding too many layers underneath can make the bathroom awkwardly higher than surrounding rooms. Be sure to check with a building professional or a flooring dealer for specifics.

COMPARING FLOORING

Hardwood

Advantages. A classic hardwood floor creates a warm decor, feels good underfoot, and can be refinished. Oak is most common, with maple, birch, and other species also available.

The three basic types are narrow strips in random lengths; planks in various widths and random lengths; and wood tiles, laid in blocks or squares. Wood flooring may be factory-prefinished or unfinished, to be sanded and finished in place. "Floating" floor systems have several veneered strips

atop each backing board. In addition, you'll now find "planks" and "tiles" of high-pressure laminate that look surprisingly like the real thing.

Disadvantages. Moisture damage and inadequate floor substructure are two bugaboos. Maintenance is another issue; some surfaces can be mopped or waxed, some cannot. Bleaching and some staining processes may wear unevenly and are difficult to repair. Cost is moderate to high, depending on wood species, grade, and finish.

Stone

Advantages. Natural stone (such as slate, marble, granite, and limestone) has been used as flooring for centuries. Today, its use is even more practical, thanks to the development of efficient sealers and surfacing techniques. Stone can be used in its natural shape—known as flagstone—or cut into rectangular blocks or tiles. Generally, pieces are butted tightly together; irregular flagstones require wider grout joints.

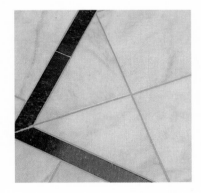

Disadvantages. The cost of masonry flooring can be quite high, though recent diamond-saw technology has lowered it considerably. Moreover, the weight of the materials requires a very strong, well-supported subfloor. Some stone is cold and slippery underfoot, though new honed and etched surfaces are safer, subtler alternatives to polished surfaces. Certain stones, such as marble and limestone, absorb stains and dirt readily. Careful sealing is essential.

Carpeting

Advantages. Carpeting cushions feet, provides firm traction, and helps deaden sound. It's especially useful to define subareas within multiuse layouts or master suites. New tightly woven commercial products are making carpeting more practical. Like resilient flooring, carpeting is available in an array of styles and materials, with prices that vary widely.

Disadvantages. Generally, the more elaborate the material and weave, the greater the problems from moisture absorption, staining, and mildew. Carpeting used in bathrooms should be short-pile and unsculptured. Woven or loop-pile wool should be confined to dressing areas. Nylon and other synthetic carpets are a wiser choice for splash zones; these are washable and hold up better in moist conditions.

Wall Coverings

BOLD, BEAUTIFUL BACKDROPS FOR YOUR DREAM BATH

In addition to the shower and tub-surround areas, your bathroom will probably include a good bit of wall space. These surfaces must be able to withstand moisture, heat, and high usage. They also go a long way toward defining the impact of your room.

Here are four popular wall treatments. You might also choose to use stone (see page 85), solid-surface materials, or other countertop choices. Glass block (page 105), whether serving as window or wall, can admit soft natural light while maintaining privacy. And fabric-upholstered walls, though they probably don't leap to mind right away, can add a dash of style and a measure of soundproofing in powder rooms or master bath areas where there's no shower or tub.

Paint

Everybody thinks of paint first. But what's best for the bathroom?

The suitable choices are latex or alkyd paint.

Latex is easy to work with, and you can clean up wet paint with soap and water. Alkyd paint (often called oil-base paint) provides high gloss and will hang on a little harder than latex; however, alkyds are trickier to apply and require cleanup with mineral spirits. Usually, the higher the resin content, the higher the gloss; so look for products labeled gloss, semi-gloss, or satin if you want a tough, washable finish.

Faux (literally, false) finishes produce the patterns or textures of materials other than plain paint. In one version, many closely related pastels are built up in subtle layers with brush strokes, by stippling, or with a sponge. Other faux treatments might layer paint textures and/or multiple colors to mimic anything from stenciled wallpaper to ancient stone.

Ceramic tile

Tough, water-resistant tile is always a good choice for a bathroom, and the range of colors, textures, shapes, and sizes opens up many creative possibilities.

Wall tiles are typically glazed and offer great variety in color and design. Generally less heavy than floor tiles, their relatively light weight is a plus for vertical installation. Made by machine, these tiles have crisp, precise shapes—they're usually set closely together, with thin (1/16-inch) grout lines. Common sizes include 3 by 3, 4 1/4 by 4 1/4, and 6 by 6 inches; larger squares and rectangles may also be available.

Prices range from as little as 50 cents per commercial tile to $20 or more per square foot for custom colors or one-of-a-kind creations. Decorative art tiles can make striking accents in a field of less expensive wall tiles, especially in low-impact areas such as backsplashes and tub surrounds.

GLOSS WALL TILES

MATTE WALL TILES

STONE-TEXTURED WALL TILES

Many wall tile lines feature coordinated border and trim pieces. Some integrated lines include matching floor tiles, countertop tiles, and coordinated bathroom fixtures and accessories.

Remember that neither glazed wall tiles nor art tiles are waterproof on their own. Water-resistant backing, adhesive, and grout can improve performance; but for vulnerable locations like showers, it's best to choose vitreous or impervious tiles.

Wallpapers

A wallpaper for the bathroom should be scrubbable, durable, and stain resistant. Vinyl wallpapers, which come in a wide variety of colors and textures, fill the bill. New patterns, including some that replicate other surfaces (such as linen), are generally subtle. A wallpaper border can add visual punch to ceiling lines and openings.

Textile wall coverings come in many colors and textures, from casual to formal. They're usually made of cotton, linen, or other natural plant fibers or of polyester, often bonded to a paper-type backing. Grass cloth is a favorite among textile wall coverings; hemp is similar but has thinner fibers. Keep in mind that most textiles fray easily and are not washable, though most will accept a spray-on stain repellent.

Wood

Solid wood paneling—natural, stained, bleached, or painted—provides a warm ambience in country schemes. Wainscoting is traditional, with a chair rail separating wood paneling below it from the painted or papered wall above it.

Generally, solid boards have edges specially milled to overlap or inter-

lock. Hardwood boards are milled from such species as oak, maple, birch, and mahogany. Common softwoods include cedar, pine, fir, and redwood.

Moldings are also back in vogue. You'll find basic profiles at lumberyards and home centers. Specialty millwork shops are likely to have a wide selection and will often custommatch an old favorite to order.

When shopping, you'll encounter words like clear, stain-grade, and paint-grade. The molding you want depends on the finish you plan: clear finishes require the best lumber; moldings that are to be painted can be of lesser grades.

Wallpapers and borders like those shown above add soft, traditional charm. But before you choose a paper, consider the territory: hard-use areas such as family baths and kids' baths might require tougher, washable vinyl products.

WOOD WAINSCOTING

Windows and Skylights

THESE OPENINGS SHED DAYLIGHT ON YOUR NEW DESIGN

After years of timidly guarding their users' privacy, bathrooms are now taking advantage, in earnest, of available light and views.

You can use glass in different structures (windows, skylights, blocks) and finishes (clear or translucent) to bring in more daylight and views while still protecting the bathroom enclosure from the world outside.

Windows

Windows are available with frames made of wood, clad wood, aluminum, vinyl, steel, or fiberglass (a newcomer). Generally, aluminum windows are the least expensive, wood and clad wood the most costly. Vinyl- or aluminum-clad wood windows and all-vinyl windows require little maintenance.

Operable windows for bathrooms include double-hung, casement, sliding, and awning types. Which you choose depends partly on your home's style and partly on ventilation needs. Also, consider such specialty units as bays, bows, and greenhouse windows—all attractive as tub surrounds.

Many of the greatest strides in window technology are taking place in glazing. Insulating glass is made of two or more panes of glass sealed together, with a space between the panes to trap air. Low-e (low-emissivity) glass usually consists of two sealed panes separated by an air space and a transparent coating. Some manufacturers use argon gas between panes of low-e glass

to add extra insulation. Look for quality and a guarantee when choosing insulating glass: with low-quality installations, a streaky look can develop between panes.

Window shopping can require at least a passing acquaintance with some specialized jargon. For a quick glossary, see "Window Words," opposite.

Skylights

You can pay as little as $100 for a fixed acrylic skylight, about $500 for a pivot-

Among the many window styles are primed wood casement with simulated divided lights (1), wood slider with aluminum cladding and snap-on grille (2), prefinished wood casement (3), anodized aluminum slider (4), vinyl double-hung (5), wood circle with aluminum cladding (6), and aluminum octagon (7).

ing model that you crank open with a pole, or several thousand dollars for a motorized unit that automatically closes when a moisture sensor detects rain.

The most energy-efficient designs feature double glazing and "thermal-break" construction.

Fixed skylights vary in shape from square to circular; they may be flat, domed, or pyramidal in profile. Most skylight manufacturers also offer at least one or two ventilating models that open to allow fresh air in and steam and heat out. Think of rotary roof windows as a cross between windows and skylights. They have sashes that rotate on pivots on two sides of the frame, which permits easy cleaning. Unlike openable roof skylights, these are typically installed on sloping walls.

If there's space between the ceiling and roof, you'll need a light shaft to direct light to the room below. It may be straight, angled, or splayed (wider at the bottom).

Glass block

If you'd like to have some ambient daylight but don't want to lose your privacy, consider another glazing option—glass block. It provides an even, filtered light that complements many bath designs.

You can buy 3- or 4-inch-thick glass blocks in many sizes; rectangular and curved corner blocks are also available in a more limited selection. Textures can be smooth, wavy, rippled, bubbly, or crosshatched. Most block is clear, though Italian block also comes in blue, rose, and green tones, and German block comes in gold tone.

To locate glass block, look in the yellow pages under Glass—Block Structural, Etc. You may be able to special-order blocks through a regular glass or tile dealer.

WINDOW WORDS

Strange, intimidating words seem to orbit the subject of windows and their components, construction, and installation. Here's a crash course in standard window jargon, enough to help you brave a showroom, building center, or product brochure.

Apron. An applied interior trim piece that runs beneath the unit, below the sill.

Casement. A window with a frame that hinges on the side, like a door.

Casing. Wooden window trim, especially interior, added by owner or contractor. Head casing runs at the top, side casings flank the unit.

Cladding. A protective sheath of aluminum or vinyl covering a window's exterior wood surfaces.

Flashing. Thin sheets, usually metal, that protect the wall or roof from leaks near the edges of windows or skylights.

Glazing. The window pane itself—glass, acrylic plastic, or other clear or translucent material. It may be one, two, or even three layers thick.

Grille. A decorative, removable grating that makes an expanse of glass look as though it were made up of many smaller panes.

Jamb. The frame that surrounds the sash or glazing. An extension jamb thickens a window to match a thick wall.

Lights. Separately framed panes of glass in a multipane window; each light is held by muntins.

Low emissivity. A high-tech treatment that sharply improves the thermal performance of glass, especially in double-glazed windows, at little added cost.

Mullion. A vertical dividing piece; whereas muntins separate small panes of glass, mullions separate larger expanses or whole windows.

Muntin. A slender strip of wood or metal framing a pane of glass in a multipane window.

R-value. Measure of a material's ability to insulate; the higher the number, the lower your heating or cooling bills should be.

Sash. A window frame surrounding glass. It may be fixed or operable.

Sill. An interior or exterior shelf below a window unit. An interior sill may be called a stool.

U-value. Measure of the energy efficiency of all the materials in the window; the lower the U-value, the less the waste.

GLASS BLOCK

Light Fixtures

LIGHT UP THE NIGHT WITH THESE ARTIFICIAL SOURCES

WALL SCONCES

Designers separate lighting into three categories: task, ambient, and accent. Task lighting illuminates a particular area where a visual activity—such as shaving or applying makeup—takes place. Ambient (or general) lighting fills in the undefined areas of a room with a soft level of light—enough, say, for a relaxing soak in a whirlpool tub. Accent lighting, which is primarily decorative, is used to highlight architectural features or attrac-

UNDER-COUNTER ACCENT LIGHT

tive plants, to set a mood, or to provide drama.

Which fixtures are best?

Generally speaking, small and discreet are watchwords in bathroom lighting; consequently, recessed downlights are very popular. Though these fixtures, fitted with the right baffle or shield, can handle ambient, task, and accent needs alone, it's almost always better to add additional fill light.

In a larger bathroom, a separate fixture to light the shower or bath area—or any other distinct part in a compart-mentalized design—and perhaps another for reading may be appreciated. Shower fixtures should be waterproof units with neoprene seals.

Fixtures around a makeup or shaving mirror should spread light over a person's face rather than onto the mirror surface. To avoid heavy shadows, it's best to place mirror lights at the sides, rather than only above the mirror. Wall sconces flanking the mirror not only provide effective light, but offer an opportunity for a stylish design statement.

And just for fun, why not consider decorative strip lights in a toe-space area or a row of hidden uplights atop wall cabinets? These low-key accents help provide a wash of ambient light and can also serve as safe, pleasant night lights.

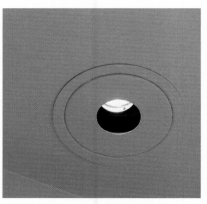

DOWNLIGHT WITH PINHOLE APERTURE

Light bulbs and tubes

Light sources can be grouped in general categories according to the way they produce light.

INCANDESCENT LIGHT. This light, the kind used most frequently in our homes, is produced by a tungsten thread that burns slowly inside a glass bulb. A-bulbs are the old standbys; R and PAR bulbs produce a more controlled beam; silvered-bowl types diffuse light. A number of decorative bulbs are also available.

INCANDESCENT/FLUORESCENT MIRROR LIGHTS

Low-voltage incandescent lighting is especially useful for accent lighting. Operating on 12 or 24 volts, these lights require transformers, which are sometimes built into the fixtures, to step down the voltage from standard 120-volt household circuits.

Low-voltage fixtures are relatively expensive to buy. But in the long run, low-voltage lighting can be energy- and cost-efficient if carefully planned.

FLUORESCENT LIGHT. Fluorescent tubes are unrivaled for energy efficiency. They also last far longer than incandescent bulbs. In some energy-conscious areas, general lighting for new bathrooms must be fluorescent.

Older fluorescent tubes have been criticized for noise, flicker, and poor color rendition. Electronic ballasts and better fixture shielding against glare have remedied the first two problems; as for the last one, manufacturers have developed fluorescents in a wide spectrum of colors, from very warm (about 2,700 degrees K) to very cool (about 6,300 degrees K).

QUARTZ HALOGEN. These bright, white sources are excellent for task lighting, pinpoint accenting, and other dramatic accents. Halogen is usually low-voltage but may use standard line current. The popular MR-16 bulb creates the tightest beam; for a longer reach and wider coverage, choose a PAR bulb. There's an abundance of smaller bulb shapes and sizes to fit pendant fixtures and strip lights.

Halogen has two disadvantages: its high initial cost and its very high heat production (halogen bulbs must be used in fixtures appropriate for them). Be sure to shop carefully. Some fixtures are not UL-approved.

COMPARING LIGHT BULBS AND TUBES

INCANDESCENT

A-Bulb
Description. Familiar pear shape; frosted or clear.
Uses. Everyday household use.

T—Tubular
Description. Tube-shaped, from 5" long. Frosted or clear.
Uses. Cabinets, decorative fixtures.

R—Reflector
Description. White or silvered coating directs light out end of funnel-shaped bulb.
Uses. Directional fixtures; focuses light where needed.

PAR—Parabolic aluminized reflector
Description. Similar to auto headlamps; special shape and coating project light and control beam.
Uses. Recessed downlights and track fixtures.

Silvered bowl
Description. A-bulb, with silvered cap to cut glare and produce indirect light.
Uses. Track fixtures and pendants.

Low-voltage strip
Description. Like Christmas tree lights; in strips or tracks, or encased in flexible, waterproof plastic.
Uses. Task lighting and decoration.

FLUORESCENT

Tube
Description. Tube-shaped, 5" to 96" long. Needs special fixture and ballast.
Uses. Shadowless work light; also indirect lighting.

PL—Compact tube
Description. U-shaped with base; 5¼" to 7½" long.
Uses. In recessed downlights; some PL tubes include ballasts to replace A-bulbs.

QUARTZ HALOGEN

High intensity
Description. Small, clear bulb with consistently high light output; used in halogen fixtures only.
Uses. Specialized task lamps, torchères, and pendants.

Low-voltage MR-16— (mini-reflector)
Description. Tiny (2"-diameter) projector bulb; gives small circle of light from a distance.
Uses. Low-voltage track fixtures, mono-spots, and recessed downlights.

Low-voltage PAR
Description. Similar to auto headlight; tiny filament, shape, and coating give precise direction.
Uses. To project a small spot of light a long distance.

Finishing Touches

ACCENTS AND ACCESSORIES COMPLETE THE PICTURE

In bathroom design, as in life in general, it's sometimes the little things that count. Don't forget to plan in those subtle amenities that can furnish delightful finishing touches.

Accessory lines are more complete than ever; some towel bars, hooks, and tissue holders even correspond with faucet handles on sinks, tubs, and showers. Additional matchables may include soap dishes, toothbrush holders, cup holders, cabinet pulls (see page 82), switch plates, mirrors, light fixtures, and wall tiles. And how about

OPTICAL MAKEUP MIRROR

a pedestal sink or bathtub that's part of the same collection?

Other popular amenities include adjustable makeup mirrors (typically 3x or 5x power), with or without optical glass and internal illumination; shaving mirrors for the shower; heated towel-bar warmers or "radiators" (see pages 98–99); and home-entertainment components (TVs, built-in speakers, control panels wired to remote audio systems).

A well-stocked bath showroom displays a dazzling array of accessories.

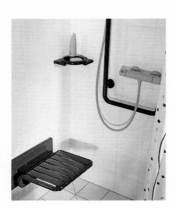

BARRIER-FREE GRAB BARS

In addition to fine design and craftsmanship, this bathroom gains visual coherence from an integrated product line. Coordinated components extend from fixtures—tub, toilet, and sink—to wall lights, mirror, shelves, and wall tiles.

design credits

91 (top). Design: Harrison Design. Contractor: Lucas Construction. Marble fabricator: Boris Cobra. 91 (bottom). Interior designer: Lequita Vance-Watkins/adVance Design of Carmel. 92 (top). Architect: Remick Associates Architects-Builders, Inc. Interior designer: Gary Hutton Design Inc. 92 (bottom). Jacuzzi Whirlpool Bath. 93. Architect: Raymond L. Lloyd. Design: Michael Assum/Mark Twisselman. 94 (top). Architect: Remick Associates Architects-Builders, Inc. 94 (bottom). The Bath & Beyond. 95. The Bath & Beyond. 95 (spray-bar). Architect: Buff, Smith & Hensman. Designer: Schlesinger Associates.

Toilets and Bidets
96. American-Standard, Inc. 97 (top). The Plumbery. 97 (bottom). The Bath & Beyond.

Ventilation
98. Architect: Remick Associates Architects-Builders, Inc. 99 (top left and right). Architect: Remick Associates Architects-Builders, Inc. 99 (bottom). The Bath & Beyond.

Flooring
100 (resilient). Designer: Gary Hutton Design. 100 (ceramic). Architect: Remick Associates Architects-Builders, Inc. 101(wood).Architect: Peter C. Rodi/Designbank. 101 (stone). Interior designer: Osburn Design. 101 (carpet). Designer: Diane Johnson Design.

Wall Coverings
102. Ann Sacks Tile & Stone. 103 (top). Laura Ashley Inc. 103 (bottom). Architect: Remick Associates Architects-Builders, Inc

Light Fixtures
106 (sconces). Architect: J. Allen Sayles. 106 (under-counter). Interior designer: Marilyn Riding Design. 106 (downlight). Architect:

House + House of San Francisco. Interior designer: Osburn Design. 106 (mirror lights). Interior designer: Osburn Design.

Finishing Touches
108 (brab bars). Hewi, Inc. 108 (showroom). The Plumbery. 109. Architect: Carson Bowler/Bowler & Cook Architects. Design: Rainer Concepts Ltd.

Design Credits
110. Interior designer: Susan Christman. Cabinetmaker: Phil Garcia Elements. 111. Architect: Morimoto Architects.

PHOTOGRAPHERS

Unless noted, all photographs are by Philip Harvey.
American Standard, Inc.: 87 top left and middle right, 96.
Alexis Andrews: 47 bottom.
Charles Callister: 32 top.
Grey Crawford: 54 bottom.
Delta Faucet Co.: 89 middle left.
Jamie Hadley: 3 (towels).
Hewi, Inc: 108 grab bars.
James Frederick Housel: 62 bottom. Jacuzzi Whirlpool Bath: 90 top, 92 bottom. Kohler Co.: 87 bottom left. Jane Lidz: 37 top.
David Duncan Livingston: 19, 26, 41, 53 top, 59 bottom, 76, 77.
Stephen Marley: 85 middle.
Jack McDowell: 101 (top.
Andrew McKinney: 46.
Mark Samu: 17 (courtesy Hearst Magazines), 40 bottom, 49 top (courtesy Hearst Magazines).
Tim Street-Porter: 28 bottom, 59 top, 60, 63. Bob Swanson: 42 bottom. Dominique Vorillon: 1, 30-31, 65, 78. David Wakely: 29. Al Webber: 55. Alan Weintraub: 109. Tom Wyatt: 99, 100 bottom, 101 bottom.

index

Page numbers in **boldface** refer to photographs